Sean Ingram

POETIC PRAYERS

OF A FALLEN ANGEL

In Loving Memory of

My love ones that I've lost during the journey

My mother, Delores Ingram Franklin
My great-grandmother, Adell Lewis
My uncles, Joe and Phillip Ingram
My lil' god-brother, Kendrick Best

I wish you could be here, cause it ain't the same without you.

Special Thanks to:
Alberta Sutton, Theresa Edwards & Omar Tyree

Thank you for your inspiration, and words of wisdom.

Published by
Sean Ingram, Inc.
P.O. Box 28131
Raleigh, NC 27611

Library of Congress
ISBN: 0-9749049-0-2

Printed in the United States of America

Acknowledgements

First and foremost, I would like to thank God because I know that without him, none of this would be possible. God, I know that I am, only because of you. To my grandmother, Retha Mae, know that I love you more than I love myself, and I'm sorry for all of the tears that I may have caused to fall from your eyes. To my mother and little brother, Delores and Dedrian, thank you for always believing in my visions, and always standing by my side through thick and thin. To my grandfather, Leroy, thank you for being a father to me, when mine was nowhere to be found. To my aunt and uncle, aunt Bob and uncle George, know that I truly do appreciate all that you have done for me, and know that I will love you always. To my beautiful nieces, Taisha and Shaila, you are my sunshine in my darkest moments, you are my breath of fresh air and the reason why I smile, know that I love you both with all of my heart. To my cousin Corey and wife Juaranita, I will thank you always for the encouragement that you have given me to follow my dreams, no matter how many obstacles that I may have to overcome. To my cousin, Ebony Janath, thank you for always bringing a smile into my heart even when I have faced so much heartache and pains, know that I love you cuz. To my god-brother and god-sister, Demorris and Lakeecia, thank you for all of your support through the many years, and thank you for being you.   To the rest of my family, The Williams and Howard family, know that I love each of you from the bottom of my heart. And last but not least I want to thank my Leventon Chapel Church family, for always staying in my corner even when I was fighting a lost battle.

Much Love, to all of my partners, Hulio, Bro. Best, Red, Quette, Shonte, Dwan, Wade, and Mark, know that I will always love yall.

Much Love, to all of the youth that have touched my heart and soul, know that I am always here to wipe your tears away or if you ever need a friend to talk with. One Love, to my Soul Ave crew, my Hazardous family, all of the Poets that I've ever came across and have effected my life in one way or another. And to everyone else, Peace and Blessings.

Dear God,

First and foremost, I just wanna say thank you. God I thank
you for my life and for everything that I have ever been through.
God I have seen the best of the best and the worst of the worst, and
now I know that it was all part of your plan for me. God I thank
you for every tear that I may have shed in the way of words through
the years, because I know that you didn't intentionally mean to hurt
me, but you did what was needed to make me the man that you have
destined for me to be. God I wanna thank you for never forsaking
me when it seems as if everyone else had. God so many people have
criticized me in life, but now I know that you're the only critic that
opinion matters, because I dwell in you just as you dwell in me.

God I'm sorry if my emotions have came through to be harsh
or disrespectful in my poetry, but you said that I should confess
completely and whole-heartedly, and that's what I do. God I don't
use profanity to curse your name, I use it to exclaim emotions, and
I also feel that it's my duty as a person that has been blessed to be
put in my position to reach the masses through poetry, so therefore
I say things in a way that everyone can understand, even if I have to
yell just to make sure that they heard me. Please forgive me if I was
wrong, but I write the only way I know how, which is from the heart.

God I'm sorry if you feel that I have wrongfully attacked any of your children or any of your churches in any shape, form, or fashion, but I do pray that you understand what it is that I'm really saying in my poems. God it seems as if so many saints have become "holier than thou", and just the thought of associating themselves with the sinners that really need them will taint their holy image. God it seems as if a lot of preachers just stand behind the pulpit shouting out a whole lot of nothing, and it's beginning to seem that a very few of them actually practice what they preach. God please don't think that I'm knocking all people of the ministry because you do have a faithful few that praise your name for the love of you, and just not for the love of recognition and money.

God it seems as if we are living in a hypocritical world, and if you don't feel the way they say you should feel then you will be punished. God you wouldn't believe some of the stuff that's going on in this world. We have children killing children, children having children, and to top it all God, some so called saints say that's it okay to be homosexual, not only that, but they say it's even okay to be a homosexual bishop. God I get so confused at times that I don't know what to think. God I have often feared that I may be following the wrong leaders, and instead of them leading me to heaven, they're actually leading me straight to hell.

Well God I ain't gonna keep holding you up because I know that you have a lot of other people letters to read. And I know that you have a whole world to look after, so just let me know if you need for me to be a Shepherd unto your sheep, and I will tend to them the best that I know how. God know that I love you and I will forever pray for your forgiveness, and I will forever thank you for your unconditional love and mercy.

Forever Yours,
Demont Sean Ingram

POETIC PRAYERS

OF A FALLEN ANGEL

Jeremiah 1:4-9

Then the word of the Lord came unto me saying,
Before I formed you in the belly I knew you
And before you came out of the womb I sanctified you,
And I ordained you to be a prophet unto the nations

Then I said, Ah, Lord God!
I cannot speak: because I am only a child

But then the Lord said unto me,
Don't say I am only a child:
For you shall go to all that I shall send you,
And whatsoever I command of you to speak
Don't be afraid of their faces:
For I am with you to deliver you, said the Lord

Then the Lord put forth his hand, and touched my mouth,
And the Lord said unto me,
Behold, I have put my words in your mouth

God sometimes I still can't understand
Why you have chosen me to help spread your word
Knowing that I'm nothing more than a child
You have still chosen me to be a shepherd unto your herd

And to be honest with you God I really don't know
If I can handle the responsibilities that comes with this position
And I know that you'll never give me more than I could bear
But God I'm still gonna need you
To make it through this mission

But God if it's your will
Then I'll speak these poetic prophecies until the day I die
And I pray that you give me the answers to any questions
Just incase somebody should happen to ask me why

God I pray that you give me the knowledge, and the wisdom
So I may completely understand what's written in your word
And God give me the courage to testify my own sins
So that I may lead by example, and not just by what I've heard

God bless me with compassion
So that I may speak completely from the heart
And shield me with your wings
So that I may be protected from those
Who'll try to tear me apart

God cover me with your blood
Just as you did when I was still in my mother's belly
And I promise you that no matter when or where
I will gladly go and speak whatever words that you tell me

I have taken you from the ends of the earth,
And called you from the chief men, and said unto you
You are my servant; I have chosen you, and not cast you away

Fear not; for I am with you:
Do not be dismayed; for I am your God:
I will strengthen you, and I will help you
I will hold you up with my right hand of righteousness

They that were angry with you
Shall be ashamed and confused:
They shall be as nothing;
And they that argue with you shall die

You shall search for them, and not find them
Even them that challenged you,
And them that are at war with you
Shall be as nothing, and as a thing of nonexistent

For I the Lord your God will hold your right hand,
Saying to you, Fear Not; I will help you

God my heart has been broken
And mine eyes have been filled with tears
So therefore my visions have been blurred
And my sweet dreams have been corrupted by fears

God my friends have forsaken me
And my freedoms have been taken away
So therefore, I cry out to you with no voice
But I know that you'll hear my silent cry when I pray

God my peace of mind has been terrorized
And my spirits have been concord by flesh
God I pray that you protect this prisoner of war
So that I may be able to bear all of my strains and stress

God I lift my hands up towards you
As I stand here just as naked as I came
Thanking you for my knowledge, wisdom, and understanding
Which will always be more valuable to me
Than fortune and fame

God the devil has tested my faith
But I thank you for all of my heartache and pains
Even when the devils hate bound me by shackles
Your love allowed me to mentally break free from his chains

God know that I am your soldier
And I will serve you until the very end
God know that I love you
And I thank you for being my father and my closest friend

My God, my God,
Why have you forsaken and neglected me?

Why are you so far from helping me,
And the words of my intense plea?

O my God, I cry in the daytime, but you do not hear me;
And even in the night, I cannot stay silent

Our fathers trusted in you:

They trusted you, and you delivered them

They cried unto you,
And they were delivered
They trusted in you,
And were not confused

So why do I fell confused and forsaken?

God you said that you would never forsake me
So why in my time of need, you're no where to be found

God I've been calling day and night
And you still haven't answered
So now the devil got me convinced,
That you no longer want me around

God I'm trying to confess my sins to you
But it's like you refuse to accept this sinner's plea
So now I find myself calling on Jesus, cause he said that
Whosoever believed in God, should also believe in me

God I have sincerely trusted in your word
So I refuse to believe that you have left me alone
But God I must admit that I'm becoming a tad bit afraid
Because I know that I can't make it on my own

God I truly do need you
So please don't forsaken me now
And I know that Jesus is the way, the truth, and the life
But why want he tell me when, where, who, and how

God I'm just a lost child with no direction or guidance
That's trying to find his way back on his own
And I know that you have prepared
A place for me in your kingdom
So please guide and direct me, so I may find my way home

God please order my steps in your word
So that I may walk with my head held high
Cause it's hard keeping my head above the troubled waters
But God I refuse to give up and die

Let not your heart be troubled:
If you believe in God, believe also in me

In my Father's house are many mansions:
If it were not so, I would have told you,
I'll go and prepare a place for you
But if I go and prepare a place for you,
I will come again and receive you myself,
So that where I am, you may be there also,
No matter if you know where I go, or the way

Then Thomas said unto the Lord,
We don't know where you are going,
So how can we know the way?

Jesus said unto him,
I am the way, the truth, and the life:
No man will come unto my Father, but by me alone

My God I'm lost right now
And I need you to help me find my way
I've done all I know to do in these cold streets
So now I lift my hands up to you and pray

And I know that I only call on you when I need you
God please forgive me, cause I know it ain't right
Especially when you have shared your love with me
And even in my darkest hours God, you have given me light

But what am I to do God
When life itself becomes too much for me to bear
And I don't mean to bother you all the time my God
But it seems as if you're the only one to really care

God my heart is torn,
But my tears won't fall
Cause even as a child
I've never learned to mourn

So now that I'm a man I cry silently,
Praying that you direct me safely
To wherever it is that I'm supposed to be going

And I know that I ran away from you, so please forgive me
Cause I'm just a lost child that's trying to find his way home
And I know I may holla that me against the world shit
But the truth is that I need you God,
Cause I can't make it on my own

Psalm 143:1-4

Hear my prayer, O Lord,
And listen to my humbling request:
And answer me in your faithfulness,
And also in your righteousness

Please do not judge me as your servant:
For in your sight no man living should be justified

The devil has persecuted my soul:
He has also brought my life down to the ground;
He has made me stay in the darkness,
As those that have been long dead

Therefore my sprite is overwhelmed within me;
But my heart seems lifeless

God it seems for me just to make it through the day
I must beg and borrow
So now when I pray at night
I ask that you Take me in my sleep,
So I don't have to face tomorrow

And God I'm sorry if I haven't lived my life
The way that you wanted me too
But please understand
That I only did what I felt I had to do

God I've tried and tried
And I have cried and cried
But to be honest with you God
I'm just sick and tired of being sick and tired

And God I know
That suicide is by far the greatest sin
But only you and I know God
The pain that my young heart holds within

Cause it seems that everything
I do and say is always wrong
And God I do thank you for giving me life
But sometimes I just don't know if this is where I belong

So God I ask that you take me
So that I may not have to take myself
But please understand that I will if I have too
Cause I refuse to let the devil breathe my last breath

The Lord is my light and my salvation;
Whom shall I fear?

The Lord is the strength of my life;
Whom shall I be afraid?

When the wicked, even my enemies and my foes,
Came upon me to eat up my flesh, they stumbled and fell

Though an host should encamp against me,
My heart shall have no fear:
Though war should rise against me,
I will be confident

I have desired one thing of the Lord that I will seek after
That I may dwell in the house of the Lord
All the days of my life,

To behold the beauty of the Lord,
And to enquire in his temple

God I just wanna say thank you
I wanna thank you for all that I have, and all that I don't
God you gave me every thing I need to make it in life
And some things I didn't even want

God you gave me my family and my friends
And also my good health with talents to do most all
You even gave me my hard times God
Just to let me know that if I wasn't careful, I could also fall

And to be honest with you God
I've faced some times in my life, I just didn't know what to do
But at times it seemed as if I gave up my God
I didn't, I just left it up to you

So if it seems as if my hand's grip is slipping from you God
It's not because I'm letting go,
It's because the devil is pulling my leg
And I know it's because of your sunshine that I live
But the devil's gray skies got me feeling that I'm better off dead

He even got me calling my grandmother a liar
Cause she promised me
"That joy would cometh in the morning light"
But God I haven't yet lost faith in you
So therefore, I know everything will be alright

So if it's your will my God,
I'll never stop, I'll just keep on keeping on
And I pray that I'll see you when I get there
So until then, know that I love you, forever yours, Lil' Sean

Matthew 10:16-22

I send you out as a sheep amongst the wolves:
Because you are as wise as the serpents,
And as harmless as the doves

But be aware of all men:
Because they will deliver you up to their councils
And they will punish you in their congregations
And you shall be brought before governors
And kings for my sake,
To testify against them and the Gentiles

And when they deliver you up
Don't think about how or what you should say:
Because it shall be given to you
In the same hour that you must speak
Because it is not you who will be speaking,
But the Spirit of your Father will be speaking through you

The brother shall deliver up his brother to death,
And the father shall deliver up his child:
And the children shall rise up against their parents,
And cause them to be put to death

You shall be hated by all men for my name's sake,
But he that endures to the end shall be saved

God I never claimed to be the g.o.a.t
But I always knew that I was your lamb
And I now realize that being thrown amongst the wolves
At a young age only made me the man that I am

But sometimes I wonder why out of all the poets in the world
Why it is that you have personally chosen me
And why have you blessed me to paint poetic pictures
For every man, woman, and child to see

But I guess that's why instead of being born with a
Silver spoon in my mouth, I was born with a pen in my hand
And what many thought to be only as chicken scratch
Were actually scriptures that only you could understand

God even though I try to uplift your name when I speak
Many say that I'm arrogant,
And have labeled me as being conceited
But God I can't help if I'm overwhelmed with your joy
Cause I'm just giving them what you told me they needed

But God as long as you keep me breathing
I'll keep speaking your word until my very last breath
And they can throw stones at me all they want
Cause I know that you'll be protecting me from death

God just allow me to be your vessel
And I'll make sure that every ear hears my voice
God give me the courage to testify my own sins
So that they may understand why it is that I rejoice

Psalm 27:7-14

Hear, O lord, when I cry with my voice:
Have mercy on me, and answer me
When you said, *Seek my face*;
My heart said to you, Lord I will seek your face

Please don't hide your face far from me;
And please don't put your servant away in anger:
For you have been my help, do not leave me, nor forsake me
O God of my salvation

When my father and my mother forsake me,
Then the Lord will take me up

O Lord, teach me your way, and lead me in the plain path
Because of mine enemies
Deliver me not over unto the will my enemies:
False witnesses are risen up against me,
And such as breathe out cruelty

I had fainted, unless
I had believed to see the goodness of the Lord
In the land of the living
Wait on the Lord: be of good courage,
And he will strengthen your heart: just wait on the Lord

God

Sean I am your father, and I love you because you are my son
So that's why I'll give you the directions to find heaven,
When all is done

Sean

But God it's so dark, and my path is very hard to see

God

Sean the light is near,
So just continue to keep walking towards me

Sean

But God it's so cold, and now it's beginning to rain

God

Don't worry my son, I'll protect so that you may bear the pain

Sean

But God I'm so tired, and I feel as if I just can't carry on

God

Hold on just a little longer,
I promise you that the storm is almost gone

Sean

God I can see and feel the sunshine, so I know that I'm close
But you haven't told me just what it is
That I should be looking for

God

Sean you will come upon a gate, take the key and open it
And I will be patiently waiting for you inside at heavens door

I heard a great voice out of heaven saying,
Behold, the tabernacle of God is with men,
And he will dwell with them,
And they shall be his people,
And God himself shall be with them,
And he shall be their God

God shall wipe away all tears from their eyes;
And there shall be no more death, neither sorrow, nor crying
Neither shall there be any more pain:
The former things will pass away

He that sat upon the throne said,
Behold, I make all things new, and he said unto me, Write:
For these words are true and faithful

And he said unto me, It is done;
I am Alpha and Omega, the beginning and the end
I will give to him that is a thirst
Of the fountain of the water of life freely

He that overcomes shall inherit all things;
And I will be his God, and he shall be my son

God I know that the clock is steadily ticking
But it seems as if time is standing still
And I know that Jesus is the way, the truth, and the life
But it seems as if the devil has taken my will

God it's like my heart cries out
But there's no one around to wipe away my tears
And all of my sweet dreams become nightmares
Because I still haven't learned to let go of my childhood fears

God I'm even afraid to daydream
Because I'm afraid of the visions that I might see
I'm afraid that I might release these demons in the form of tears
So that's why I cry through everybody else that's around me

So God I ask you also
Who will cry for the little boy that cries inside of I
Who will mend my broken heart, wipe away my tears
And show me why it's better to live than to die

Who will ease my heartache and pain
And stand by my side, no matter what I may go through
God I don't mean to discredit anyone
But I know that no one will do for me, what you will do

God I pray that you give me the endurance
That I may keep overcoming these obstacles
That stand in my way
And continue to use me as your vessel
That I may speak whatever words you want me to say

Only if I knew where it is, that I could find God
I would order my case before him,
And fill my mouth with arguments
I would know the words which he would answer me,
And understand what he would say to me

Will God plead against me with his great power?

No; but he will strengthen me
The righteous might dispute him;
So I may be delivered from my judge forever

I go forward to the to the east, but he is not there;
And backward to the west, but I cannot perceive him
I go left to the north, where he works, but I can't find him:
He hides himself to my right in the south,
So that I cannot see him

But he knows the way that I have taken:
When he had tried me
So I should come out as gold

God I don't mean to be the devils advocate
But it seems to me, as if the good always finishes last
And to be honest with you God, I'm in it to win it
So I can't be half steppin',
Cause the world is moving too damn fast

God please correct me if I'm wrong
But it seems as if millionaires no longer wear suits and ties
And if they do, they gotta have on a pair of gators
Cause they're pimpin' everything from athletes to church tithes

God what kind of world are we living in when
My spiritual male role model is married to another man
God please bless me with your knowledge and wisdom
Before I become mislead by the things that I don't understand

God I've already read the book of Genesis
So I know shit like that is wrong
Just as them girls who strip on Saturday night
And then stand in church on Sunday morning leading a song

God I'm just searching for the truth
But it seems as if you are so far away from me
And this world got me so confused
I don't even know who it is that I'm suppose to be

God please excuse me if I'm out of place
But I gotta say what's on my mind and what my heart truly feel
Cause it was you who said that I should confess completely
So anything less than the truth, wouldn't be real

Unto you I will cry O lord my rock;
Don't be silent to me,
For I am worried that if you are silent to me,
I become like them that go down in the pit

Hear the voice of my humble prayers, when I cry unto you,
When I lift my hands up towards your holy shrine
Don't draw me away with the wicked,
And with the workers of iniquity,
Which speaks peace to the neighbors,
But evil is in their hearts

Give to them according to their deeds,
And according to the wickedness of their endeavors:
Give to them after the work of their hands;

Render to them their desert
Because they don't regard the works of the Lord,
Nor the operation of his hands,
He shall destroy them, and not build them up

God I don't mean to question your plan
But I still can't understand why so many young people must die
And why is it that our children must shed tears
Without anybody there to wipe the tears from their eye

God it seems as if we're living in a world
That produces more widows than wives
And instead of kids carrying books to school
They're now carrying guns and knives

God we got kids who think it's cool
To bust slugs for the love of drug money
They're laughing on the outside, while crying on the inside
But this shit ain't no joke God, and it ain't a damn thang funny

God everybody's feeling like they're stuck in between
A rock and a hard place with their back against the wall
And some are so tired of being at rock bottom,
They commit suicide
Cause they feel like it ain't nowhere else for them to fall

God it's fucked up here, so please hear my cry
Even though my heart may not be completely free of sin
And I know that the blind can't lead the blind
So please give me the vision
So I can be ready when you come again

God please give me the words so that I'll know what to say
To the children that my voice may touch
And if I should happen to fall along the way
Please don't forsake me, but stand by me as my crutch

This is the message that we have heard of him,
And declared to you,

God is the light,
And in him is no darkness at all

If we say we fellowship with him, and walk in darkness,
We are liars, and have not told the truth:
But if we walk in the light, for that he is in the light

We have fellowshipped with one another
And the blood of his son Jesus Christ cleans us from all sins

If we say that we have no sins, we deceive ourselves,
And the truth will not be in us
But if we confess our sins,
He is faithful and quick to forgive us,
And cleanse us from all that is unrighteous

If we say that we have not sinned,
We make him a liar, and his word is not in us

God I have walked through the darkest valleys
With you on one side of me, and the devil on the other

God I got confused between right and wrong
Cause I've learned that all is fair
In the streets and in the struggle

God I have endured the pain
I've even taken some showers in the cold rain

And though I've had thoughts of committing suicide God
It's only because of your grace and mercy
That I've still maintained

So now God I baptize my unborn children
In the many tears that I've shed

And since I no longer need to get high to get bye
I pour out my liquor for all my fallen soldiers that lay dead

God I never meant to become a burden
Nor did I mean to be any harm

But to survive in a cold world such as this
I gotta do what I gotta do in order to stay warm

God I pray that you forgive me
For all of the wrong that I've done

And I pray that you will always love me
For you are my father, and I am your son

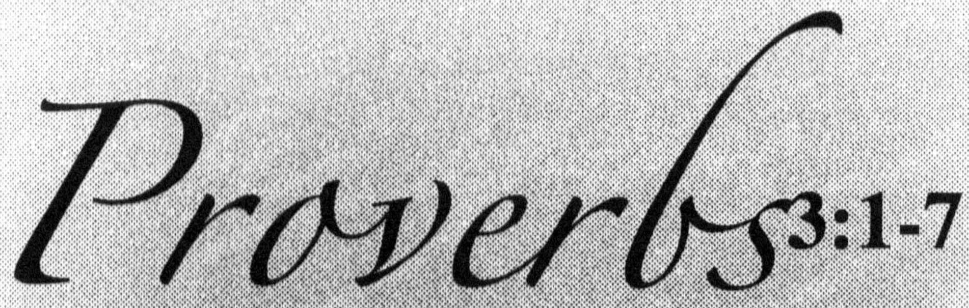

My son, don't forget my law;
But let your heart keep my commandments

So that long days, long life,
And peace should be given unto you

Don't let mercy and truth forsake you:
Bind them around your neck,
And write them in the tablet of your heart

So that you may find favor and good understanding,
In the sight of God and man

Trust in the Lord with all your heart;
And do not lean on your own understanding
In all your ways acknowledge God,
And he shall direct your paths

Don't be wise in your own eyes:
But fear the Lord, and depart from evil

God where did I go wrong
And where did my roads cross paths
God, why was I so happy when I had nothing
But even happier when I lost all that I had

God what is the moral of this story
And what is it that I'm suppose to learn from this lesson plan
God I pray that you give me the knowledge and wisdom
So I may comprehend the things that I don't understand

God I pray that you teach me
Everything that you want me to learn
God give me the courage to stand my ground
Even when people tell me that it's none of my concern

God I pray that you open my eyes
To whatever it is that you want me to see
God allow me the versatility
So I can be whoever it is that you want me to be

God allow me to be a vessel for you
So I may spread your word throughout the earth
God I pray that you allow me to live after death
And I pray that you allow me to be reborn even after birth

God I pray that you keep me in your arms
Cause even us thugs and hustlers need a hug
And I pray that you continue to dwell in my heart
Cause I know that I'm worthless without your love

Psalm 25:14-21

The secret of the Lord is with them that fear him;
And he will show them his written promise

My eyes are forever towards the Lord;
For he shall pluck my feet out of the net

Turn unto me, and have mercy on me;
For I am desolate and afflicted

The troubles of my heart are enlarged:
Please bring me out of my distress

Look upon my affliction and pain; and forgive all my sins
Consider my enemies; for there are many;
That hates me with cruel hatred

God keep my soul, and deliver me:
Let me be not ashamed; for I put my trust in you
Let integrity and uprightness preserve me;

For I wait on you

God I have watched my whole life pass me by
In the reflection of my grandmother's tears
And God I pray that she forgives me
For all of the pain that I've brought her
Through the many years

God I pray that she forgives me
For all of the shame that I've brought into her life
And I pray that she forgives me
For all of the unnecessary strains and strife

God I pray that you will also forgive me
For I have not honored my mom or dad
But how can you honor the parents
That you felt you never had

God please forgive me
For leading my brothers in the wrong direction
And God please forgive me
For embracing my sister with nothing but neglection

God I pray that you forgive me
For all of the sins that I may have done
And I'm sorry if you feel that you've made a mistake
By choosing me to be your poetic chosen one

God I pray that you give me a second chance
And forgive me for all of the sins that I've done once before
God I pray that you anoint me as a man
And allow me to go and sin no more

1 Corinthians
13:1-7

Though I speak with the tongues of men and of angels,
Without compassion,
I have become as a sounding brass, or a tinkling cymbal

And though I have the gift of prophecy,
And understand all mysteries, and all knowledge;
And though I have all faith, that I could remove mountains
Without compassion, I am nothing

And though I apply all my goods to feed the poor,
And though I give my body to be burned,
Without compassion, it profits me nothing

Compassion endures long, and is kind;
Compassion isn't envious, and doesn't brag on itself,
And isn't puffed up
Compassion does not behave inappropriate,
Nor seeks what's not hers,
And is not easily provoked, and thinks of no evil

Do not rejoice in the wicked, but rejoice in the truth;
Bear all things, believe all things, hope all things,
And endure all things

God my heart bleeds for those
Who are lost in a world full of sin
And my eyes cry rivers for those who
Search for you, but don't know where to begin

God my tongue paints poetic pictures
For those who may feel that they have no voice
And God I speak for those who find a life in crime
Cause they feel like they ain't got no other choice

God I speak for the kids who get off the school bus hungry
And there is no one even at home
I speak for the kids who do badly in school
Cause they gotta figure out their homework on their own

God I speak for the college girls who strip at night
Just to feed their child, or to pay their tuition
God I speak for those who always extend an helping hand
But when they need help, it seems as if everyone is missing

God I speak for those who are now just
Living to die, and have stopped dying to live
I speak for those who gave it all they had
And now feel that they ain't got no more to give

God I speak for those people
Cause I feel that's what you have chosen for me to do
And as long as I have breath in my lungs
I will forever speak the words that you tell me too

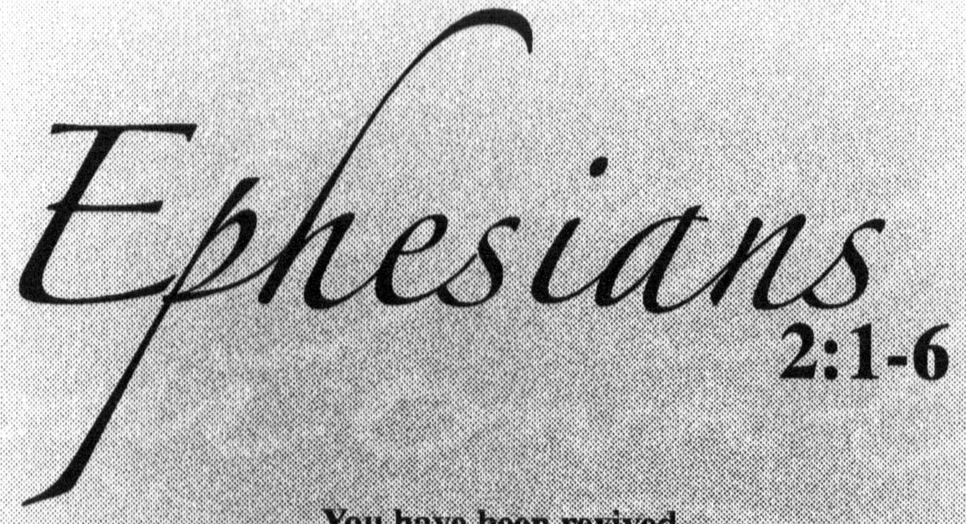

You have been revived,
Though you once were dead in violations and sins
Where in the past you've walked according to
The course of the world,

According to the prince of the power of the air,
The spirit that now works in the children of disobedience
Among all of those we have conversed
With in the lusts of our flesh,
Fulfilling the desires of the flesh and of the mind;
And naturally the children of great anger, even as others

But God, who is rich in mercy,
For his great love is why he loved us,
Even when we were dead in sins,
He has revived us together with Christ,
(by grace you are saved)

And has raised us up together, and made us sit together
In the heavenly places of Christ Jesus

God it hurts me to my heart to know that
So many people of this world feed off of negativity
And now I find myself watching my back just to make sure that
My friends that are supposed to be hugging me,
Aren't actually stabbing me

God my grandmother always told me that I should look out
For my enemies, but always keep my friends in eyesight
But God I've never been the one to have a lot of friends anyway
So I always thought that I would be alright

God I've fallen and it seems as if there is
No one around to help me get back on my feet
But yet everyone wants to throw stones at me
As I hang up on a cross with nails in my hands and feet

God why do so many people
Judge those they don't even know
And why do so many people cast stones
When they don't even have a right to throw

Because God you said that
He without sins may cast the first stone
So he that cast stones with sin
Should go to hell when they're dead and gone

And God I don't wish hell on anyone
So why do so many people wish hell upon me
And why do they wanna sacrifice me on the cross
As an example for the whole world to see

Deuteronomy
32:1-5

Please listen my heavens, and I will speak;
And please hear my earth, the words of my mouth

My doctrine shall drop as the rain,
My speech shall distill as the dew,
As the small rain upon the tender herb,
And as showers upon the grass:

Because I will publish the name of the Lord:
Ascribe his greatness unto our God

He is the Rock, his work is perfect:
For all his ways are judgment:
A God of truth and without iniquity,
He is fair and right

They have corrupted themselves,
Their spot is not the spot of his children:
They are a perverse and crooked generation

God I wish that I could just close my eyes
And let time take all of my problems away
God I wish it was easy as opening my eyes
To stop all the nightmares that I have during the day

God sometimes I wish I could just read a book that would
Take my mind away to a paradise such as "never-never land"
And then maybe I could gain some knowledge on
Some of the things that I never-never seem to understand

God I wish I could just listen to Curtis Mayfield
So he can teach me what's really going on
And sometimes I wish I could build a tree house
In my family tree, so that I may never be alone

God sometimes I just wish that I could travel to
The end of the rainbow in search of my pot of gold
Or travel to the ends of the earth in search of
The fountain of youth, so that I may never grow old

God sometimes I wish I could turn back the hands of time
So that I may have known then what it is that I know now
God I wish I could wipe away the tears from every child's face
And let them know that they'll make it someway somehow

God I find myself wishing on a star
And I pray that this star never falls from the sky
Because if it does,
All my sweet dreams may leave me
Along with the tears that constantly falls from my eye

1 Corinthians
13:8-13

Compassion has never failed:
But without compassion,
Prophecies shall fail, tongues shall cease,
And knowledge shall vanish,

For we know in part, and we preach in part
But when that is perfect is to come,
Then which is in part shall be done away

When I was a child, I spoke as a child,
I understood as a child, and I thought as a child:
But when I became a man, I put away childish ways

For now we see through a glass, darkly;
But then face-to-face: now I know in part;
But then shall I know even as also I am known

And now abide faith, hope, and compassion
But the greatest of all these three is compassion

God I live my literature
Because I know that faith without works is dead
And how can I be a spiritual male role model
When I don't practice the words that I've said

God I speak from the heart
And I will only write what is real
Never will I use your name in vain
But I do use profanity to exclaim how it is that I feel

God I just hope that you understand

God I speak with the tongues of angels
But I also speak with the voice of men
And God I shed tears for all of the young souls
That are lost in this world full of sin

God I share the labor pains with all of the mothers
That have to raise their children on their own
God I toss and turn at night for all of the children
That cry themselves to sleep at night feeling all alone

God I just pray that you comfort them

God my heart bleeds for the young girls
That have been raped of their beauty from inside out
Just as my heart goes out to the young boys
Whose manhood may have been put in doubt

God I pray that you protect them
With your love and compassion

The Lord is my Shepherd, I shall not want

He makes me lie down in green pastures:
He leads me beside the still waters
He restores my soul:
He leads me in the paths,
Of the righteousness for his name's sake

Even though I walk through the valley of the shadow of death,
I will fear no evil: for God is with me;
His rod and his staff comforts me

God prepares a table for me in the presence of my enemies:
He anoints my head with oil;
And my cup overflows

Surely goodness and mercy shall follow me
All the days of my life:
And I will dwell in the house of the Lord forever

God if I never speak another word in my life
Then I just wanna thank you for the words
That I have already spoken

God I wanna thank you for all of the hearts
That you've allowed me to touch
And for all of the souls that I may have saved
And for all of the young yokes that I may have broken

God if I never write another word in my life
Then I just wanna thank you for the words
That I have already written in your name

God I just wanna thank you for blessing me
With knowledge and wisdom and understanding
Which will always mean more to me than fortune and fame

God if I never sing another song in my life
Then I just wanna thank you for being the reason why I sing

God I just wanna thank you for all of the troubled hearts
That you've allowed me to comfort
Through the joy that your songs bring

God if I never breathe another breath in my life
Then I just wanna thank you for all of the breaths
That I have already taken once before

God I just wanna thank you for giving me life
And know that I'll continue thanking you
Until I just can't breathe anymore

Beloved, if God so loved us, we should also love one another
No man has seen God at anytime
If we love one another, God dwells in us,
An his love is perfected in us

Know that we dwell in him, and him in us,
Because he has given unto us his Spirit
And we have seen and testified that the Father sent the Son
To be the Savior of the world

Whosoever shall confess that Jesus is the Son of God,
God dwells in him, and he in God
And we have known and believed the love that God has for us,

God is love; and he that dwells in love dwells in God,
And God dwells in him

Within us is our love made perfect,
That we may have boldness in the Day of Judgment:
Because as he is, so are we in this world

God how can I turn my back on you now
When you have never once turned your back on me
And why would I stop looking towards the heavenly skies
When it was you who opened my eyes so that I can see

God why would I walk away from you now
When I know in my heart that I'm nothing without you
And how could I not praise your name
When you're responsible for everything that I do

God how can I not say my prayers at night
Especially when you've allowed me to make it through the day
And how could I not thank you in the morning
When it was you who sent me out on my way

God why wouldn't I run and tell others about you
After all of the great things that you have done for me
And why wouldn't I continue to have faith
When you allowed me to be who I was destined to be

God why wouldn't I love you
When you have always loved me as your very own
And why should I ever doubt you
When you have never left me to be alone

God how could I not be my brother's keeper
When I know that it was you who has always kept me
And God I thank you for keeping me safe from harms way
So that I may be the man that you want me to be

There is nothing covered, that shall not be revealed;
Neither hid, that shall not bee known

Therefore whatsoever you have spoken in darkness
Shall be heard in the light;
And that which you have spoken in the ear of the closets
Shall be proclaimed upon the housetops

I say unto you my friends,
Don't be afraid of them that kill the body,
Because after that it's no more that they can do

But I will forewarn you of whom you shall fear:
Fear him, which after he has killed has power to cast into hell;
I say unto you, Fear him

Are not five sparrows sold for two farthings,
And not one of them is forgotten before God?
But even the very hairs on your head are all numbered
Fear not, because you are more valuable than many sparrows

God I know that what's done in the dark
Shall one day come into the light
And that's why I can't cover up a lie with a lie
Because I know that two wrongs will never make it right

God I have confessed my sins with you
And I just pray that you understand
God you said that you would never forsake me
So I pray that when I reach out to you
That you will take my hand

God I have written my thoughts into Books
And I have verbally expressed my concerns on CD's
I have portrayed the pains of life on TV
And I have confessed my sins on bended knees

Because I have nothing to hide

But God sometimes I wonder
Will my dark past ever see brighter days
Or will the moon continue to eclipse the sun
So that I may never be able to enjoy its rays

God you said that the truth shall set you free
So that's why I speak my mind on how I really feel
Cause if what I say in the dark will come to the light
Then I wanna make sure that everything I say is real

Because you already know what's in my heart
So therefore I may can lie to others
But I can never lie to you God

O magnify the Lord with me,
And let us glorify his name together

I sought the Lord, and he heard me,
And delivered me from all my fears

They looked unto him, and were lightened:
And their faces were not ashamed

This poor man cried, and the Lord heard him,
And saved him out of all his troubles
The angel of the lord encamped around them that fear him,
And they delivered them

Taste and see that the Lord is good:

Blessed is the man that trust in him
Fear the Lord his saints:
For there is no want to those who fear him

God I know that you blessed the child that has his own
So I pray that you bless this child that never had at all
Please keep me on a straightforward path
So that I'll never backslide
And God I pray that you'll be my crutch so that I'll never fall

God I pray that you keep my eyes on the sparrow
No matter how many people criticize me
For having a narrow mind
And God I pray that you guide me safely
Through this world of sin
So when it's all said and done, your face in heaven I will find

God I pray that you give me the strength to stand strong
Even when it seems as if
The weight of the world is on my shoulders
And God I pray that I'll be able to endure
All of this pain and suffering
When the stones that people throw at me, turn into boulders

God I pray that you give me knowledge and wisdom
That I may understand what's written in between the lines
So when I see only one set of footprints in the battlefield
I'll know you haven't left me,
But you're carrying me over the mines

God I pray that you give me direction
So that I may find heaven when all is done
And I pray that you show me my purpose in life
So that I may know why you've elected me as the chosen one

I John 4:16-21

We have known and believed the love that God has for us
God is love;
And he that dwells in love dwells in God,
And God in him

Within us is our love made perfect,
That we may have boldness in the Day of Judgment:
Because as he is, so are we in this world

There is no fear in love; but perfect love cast out fear:
Because fear has torment and agony
He that fears is not made perfect in love

We love him, because he first loved us
If a man say that he loves God, and hates his brother

He is a liar:

For he that don't love his brother who he has seen,
How can he love God who he has not seen?
This is a commandment that we have from him,
That he who loves God, should also love his brother

God I know that I should love my brother
But it's hard for me to love someone
That never once seemed to love me
God how can I love someone
That smiles in my face
But throws stones at my back
When they're in a position that I can't see

God how can I love someone
That turned their back on me
When I needed them most of all
God how can I love someone
That purposely let go of me
Just so they could watch me fall

God I am my brother's keeper
But at the same time
I wanna keep these fake ass niggas
Far away from me as I possibly can
And God I do love you with all my heart
But it's hard for me to love someone
That never once seemed to love me
God I just hope that you understand

And God please understand
That just because I don't love my brother
Doesn't mean that I hate my brother
It just means that I have washed my hands clean
And I know that you said
That I should love my neighbor and enemy
And I'll try, but I must admit that it's hard
I just hope that you understand what I mean

I say unto you,
Whosoever shall confess me before men,
The Son of God shall confess him before the angels of God:

But he that denies me before men,
Shall be denied before the angels of God

And whosoever shall speak a word against the Son of man,
Shall be forgiven:
But he who blasphemes against the Holy Ghost,
Shall not be forgiven

And when they bring you in front of the congregation,
Unto the magistrates, and the powers that be,
Have no thought on how or what things you shall answer,
Or even what you will say:

For the Holy Ghost shall teach you
What you should say with in the same hour

God I have nearly killed a man
And I don't even know why
God I have watched my only two uncles
Die of AIDS and I didn't even cry

God I have witnessed the last breath
Of my great grandmother Adell
When I was only eight years old
God I have written infinite words of poetry
But still my story goes untold

God I have recited to you
Night after night on a stage
Just hoping that you will hear my silent cry
God I have walked through the lowest valleys
But I always kept my head towards the sky

God I have trusted in my grandma Retha Mae
Trusting that she would lead me in the right direction
God I have always believed in you
Believing that you would be my protection

God I have shed so many tears
And now it seems that I just can't cry anymore
God I have paid my dues to society
For the crimes that I've committed once before

God I have asked you for forgiveness
Now that I have learned my lessons
God I have completely changed my life around
And I pray that you deliver me from my confessions

Psalm 61:1-6

Hear my cry, O God;
Attend unto my prayer

From the end of earth will I cry unto you,
When my heart is overwhelmed:
Lead me to the rock that is higher than I

For you have been a shelter for me,
And a strong tower from the enemy

I will abide in your tabernacle forever:
And I will trust in the shelter of your wings

For you, O God, have heard my vows:
And you have given me the heritage
Of those who fear your name

You will prolong the king's life:
And his years as many generations

God I pray that you wipe away the tears
That I have cried for 40 days and 40 nights

God please take these shackles from my feet
And whatever else that may try to bind me
From reaching greater heights

God place me above the clouds
Where these vultures can do me no harm

God please walk side by side with me
And always keep us arm and arm

God place me on a solid rock
So that I may stand fast on a solid foundation

God please give me peace of mind
When the devil tries to play with my imagination

God bless me with a voice
So that I may continue to sing your praise

God bless me with compassion
So that I may prolong my earthly days

God bless me with a pure heart
So that I may love others
Just as you have loved me

God bless me with understanding
So that I may understand
The blueprint that the bible is meant to show me

If you have been raised with Christ,

Seek those things which are above,
Where Christ sitteth on the right hand of God

Set your affection on things above,
Not on things on the earth

For you are dead,
And your life is hid with Christ in God

When Christ, who is our life, shall appear,
Then shall you also appear with him in glory

Mortify therefore your members which are upon the earth;
Fornication, Uncleanness, Inordinate affection,
Evil concupiscence,
And Covetousness, which is idolatry

God you can have it all
From the shoes on my feet to the clothes on my back

Because I know that I came from heaven naked
So therefore, naked is the way that I'll go back

God you can even have my voice
Because I know that it's only because of you
That I'm even able to speak

God you can even have my vision
Because other than you God
I really don't have anything that I care to seek

God you can even have my soul
Because I know that my soul needs resurrection

God you can even have my breastplate
Because my heart belongs to you God
So therefore, it needs no protection

God you can even have my lungs
Because without your air
There's nothing that my lungs can do

God you can even have my feet
Because there's nowhere for me to run God
If I'm not running in the direction of you

God you can have it all
Because without you God

I am nothing at all

Ecclesiastes
7:21-25

Take no heed unto all the words that are spoken;
Unless you hear my servant curse me:

For oftentimes your own heart also knows
That you yourself likewise have cursed others

I have proved all of this by wisdom:
I said I would be wise; but it was far from me

That which is far off, and exceedingly deep,
Who can find it out?

I applied mine heart to know, and to search,
And to seek out wisdom, and the reason of things,
And to know the wickedness of folly,
Even of foolishness and madness

God I don't doubt the purpose of the church
But I must admit
I do doubt the purpose of those
That claim to be leaders

God it seems that very few
Practice what they preach
So to me they're nothing more than
Spiritual deceivers

God I even found myself not going to church
For the fear of a so called preacher
Twisting the truth to corrupt my young mind

And God I never claimed to be a Bible scholar myself
But even common sense tells me
That the blind can't lead the blind

God I've seen Bishops and Pastors
Say that it's okay to be gay

God they're beginning to contradict the Bible
I guess next they'll be saying
That Jesus isn't the truth, the life, or the way

God I'm afraid
Because I feel that the devil has planted preachers
To lead our children in the wrong direction

So God I pray that you shield us from these demons
Because God we need your protection

Galatians

4:7-13

Wherefore thou art no more a servant, but a son;
And if a son, then an heir of God through Christ

Howbeit then, when you knew not God,
You did service unto them that by nature are no gods

But now, after that you have known God,
Or rather are known of God,
How can you turn again to the weak and beggarly elements,
Whereunto you desire again to be in bondage?

You observe days, and months, and times, and years

I am afraid of you, lest I have bestowed upon you labor in vain

Brethren, I beseech you, be as I am; for I am as you are:
You have not injured me at all

You know how through infirmity of the flesh
I preached the gospel unto you at the first

God it was you who designed the blueprint of my life
So there's nothing about me
That you don't already know

So God I pray that you guide me in your direction
Because I'm really lost right now
And I really don't know which way to go

God I pray that you cover me with your wings
So that I may not drown from all of this rain

God I pray that you comfort me with your love
So that I'll be able to bear all of this pain

God I pray that you allow the sun to shine on me
So that I may not die in a world that's so cold

God I pray that you prolong my life
So that I may have a chance to grow old

God I pray that you will walk with me on this journey
So that I may not feel that I'm walking all alone

God I pray that you continue to stand by my side
When everyone else seems to be gone

God I pray that you hear my prayers
And just as I have talked to you
You will also come and talk to me

God I pray that I will make you proud
So that you may say I've done a job well done
Being the man that you have destined for me to be

I John 2:4-8

He that said, I know him, and does not his commandments,
Is a liar, and the truth is not in him

But who so keeps his work,
In him verily is the love of God perfected:
Hereby know we that we are in him

He that said he abides in him
Should also walk,
As he walked

Brethren, I write no new commandment unto you,
But an old commandment which you had from the beginning
The old commandment is the word
Which you have heard from the beginning

Again, a new commandment I write unto you,
Which thing is true in him and in you:
Because the darkness is past, and the true light now shines

God I really am trying to be like Jesus
But I know that I have many flaws

I too even roll with my twelve apostles
But I prefer to call them my dawgs

Many may think of them as sinners
Because they all have been bound at least once
By shackles and chains

But they really do have good hearts God
They're just addicted to unlawful gains

God some people even try to test me
By provoking me to turn stones into bread

God many even try to stone me to death
Just to see if I will also be raised from the dead

God I still have the scars on my body
Where people keep throwing stones at me non-stop

And if you take a look at my back
You can still see the marks of where I refused
To pick the white man's cotton or tend to his crop

God ain't a lot changed from then and now
Because they hated on Jesus just like they still hate on me

The only difference is that they hung Jesus up on a cross
But they plan on hanging my black ass from a tree

1 Peter 2:19-25

For this is thankworthy, if a man for conscience toward God
Endure grief, and suffering wrongfully

For what glory is it, when you are buffeted for your faults,
You shall take it patiently
But if, when you do well, and suffer for it,
You take it patiently, This is acceptable with God

For even hereunto were you called:
Because Christ also suffered for us, leaving us an example,
That you should follow his steps:

Who did no sin, neither was guile found in his mouth:
Who, when he was reviled, reviled not again;
When he suffered, he threatened not;
But committed himself to him that judged righteously:

Who his own self bears our sins in his own body on the tree,
That we, being dead to sins, should live unto righteousness:
By whose stripes you were healed
For you were as sheep going astray;
But are now returned unto the Shepherd
And Bishop of your souls

God I've found that what I thought to be trial and tribulations
Was only the misunderstanding of your lessons

And God what I thought to be heartache and pain
Was only the preparation for your blessings

And those I thought to be friends
Quickly became foes

And those who I thought could be wives
Seems to have become hoes

So now God I'm confused
Because it seems as if I just don't know

God I thought that I was standing on a solid rock
But I've found myself sinking quickly in the sand

And God I can feel the devil trying to pull me under
So I pray that you continue holding on to my hand

Because God he's pulling on me so hard
My hand grip is slipping from you
But I refuse to let you go

God I wish I would've known then
What it is that I know now
But since I didn't
I guess that I gotta reap what I sow

But that's alright though
Because I've learned that
It's all a part of God's plan for me

When a righteous man turned away from his righteousness,
And committed iniquity, and died in them;
For his iniquity that he has done shall he die

Again, when the wicked man turned away from his wickedness
That he has committed, and do that which is lawful and right,
He shall save his soul alive

Because he considered,
And turned away from all his transgressions
That he has committed, he shall surely live,
And he shall not die

Yet said the house of Israel, the way of the Lord is not equal
Are not your ways unequal?

Therefore I will judge you, O house of Israel,
Every one according to his ways, saith the Lord God
Repent, and turn yourselves from all your transgressions;
So iniquity shall not be your ruin

God how can one learn to get back up again
If one has never fell

And why would one sacrifice their life for heaven
If one has never been through hell

I guess it's like yen and yuan
Because what goes up must come back down

Just as in a blink of an eye
A smile can be turned into a frown

And your tears will evaporate in time
Just like the cold rain

But as soon as them dark clouds
Cover up the sunshine again
Back comes the pain

And just because someone seems to be saint now
Doesn't mean that they once wasn't a sinner

And just because someone seems to be a loser now
Doesn't mean that they can never be a winner

Because every professional in this world
Started off in life as a beginner

Now I believe that foes can become friends
Just as I believe that Jesus rose from the grave again

So why wouldn't I believe that
Addicts, hustlers', thieves' and even killers'
Souls can be saved from sin

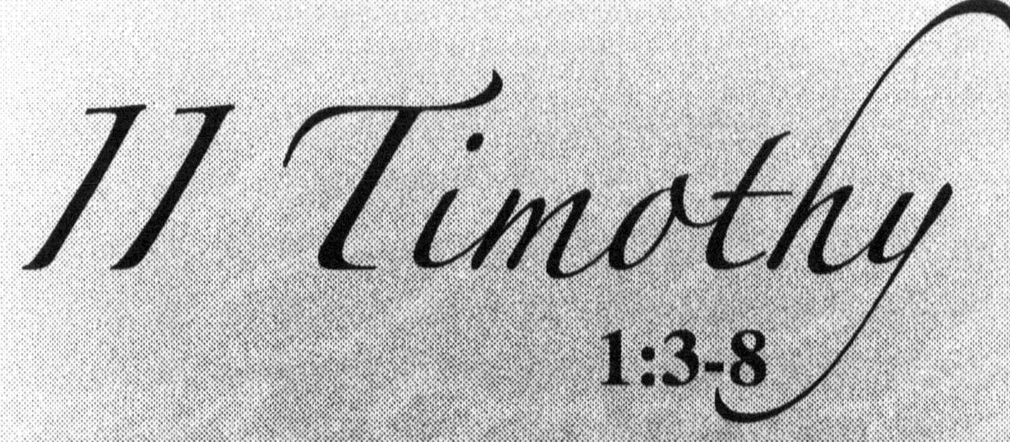

I thank God, whom I serve from my forefathers
With pure conscience, that without ceasing
I have remembrance of you in my prayers night and day;

Greatly desiring to see the being mindful of thy tears,
That I may be filled with joy;

When I call to remembrance the unfeigned faith that is in you,
Which dwelt first in thy grandmother Lois,
And thy mother Eunice;
And I am persuaded that in thee also

Wherefore I put thee in remembrance
That thou stir up the gift of God,
Which is in thee by putting on of my hands
For God hath not given us the spirit of fear;
But of power, and of love, and of a sound mind

Be not thou therefore ashamed of the testimony of our Lord,
Nor of me his prisoner: but be thou partaker of the afflictions
Of the gospel according to the power of God

God I know some may get tired of me talking spiritual
But I really don't have much to say
If I can't talk about your glory

Because I've been through so much in my life
That it's a blessing that I even have a chance
To testify through words and tell my story

And I don't claim to be a preacher
Because God knows I ain't no Bible scholar
As a matter of fact, I speak from the heart of a sinner

God all my life I thought I was a child with nothing to lose
And maybe I was, but now that I'm a man
I now realize that it didn't matter
Because without you God
I can never become a winner

God I've made a lot of mistakes in my life
But I'm not regretful
Because I guess sometimes you just gotta touch the stove
To truly learn that it burns
No matter how many people may tell you that it's hot

And God every since I was child
I've been searching for love in all of the wrong places
But how can you appreciate the one that will truly love you
If you have never known the one that will love you not

God I guess I just had to learn what love wasn't
Before I could appreciate what your love is

But now I know that God's love is mine
And my love is his

Having the understanding darkened and being alienated
From the life of God through the ignorance that is in them,
Because of the blindness of their heart:

Who being past feeling have given themselves over unto
lasciviousness, to work all uncleanness with greediness

But you have not learned Christ;

If so be that you have heard him,
And have been taught by him,
As the truth is in Jesus:

That you put off concerning
The former conversation the old man,
Which is corrupt according to the deceitful lusts;
And be renewed in the spirit of your mind;
And that you put on the new man,
Which after God is created in righteousness and true holiness

God where is my happy medium

How can I unconditionally love my brother
When I can't find any faith in him

How can I unconditionally love my sister
When I can't trust her as far as I can see

And how can I wipe away everyone's tears
When I can't seem to make everyone happy

So God where is my happy medium

Because I don't smile enough for some
But some say I smile too much

And everyone hangs on me when I stand strong
But when I sometimes get weak and fall
There's no one around that I can depend on
To stand by me and be my crutch

So God where is my happy medium

God I think people always expect me to be strong
But I guess they don't know
How much I really do need them

I guess they don't know
That I only laugh to keep from crying
Because I have no happy medium

So I ask you God, where is my happy medium

Isaiah 29:9-12

Stay yourselves, and wonder;
Cry out, and cry: they are drunken,

But not with wine; they stagger, but not with strong drink
For the Lord hath poured out upon you

The spirit of the deep sleep,
And has closed your eyes: the prophets and your rulers,
The seers hath he covered

And the vision of all is become unto you
As the words of a book that is sealed,

Which men deliver to one that is literate,
Saying, read this,
I pray thee: and he said, I cannot; for it is sealed:
And the book is delivered to him that is not literate,
Saying, read this,
I pray thee, and he said, I am illiterate

God the devil has caused my eyes to shed tears
Making it difficult to see the words in the bible
So therefore, he's making it hard for me to understand

God the devil has even placed depression in my mind
Filled my heart with loneliness
As he tries to convince me
That you no longer want to hold my hand

God the devil has even tampered with my brain
Causing me to become illiterate
So now I feel as if I cannot read your word

God the devil has even taken my memory
Causing me to forget what I've already read
And every sermon that I have already heard

God the devil has even taken my heart
So now I know nothing about love

God the devil has even drained my arteries
And filled my veins with cold blood

God the devil has even taken my eyesight
So now I find myself in the dark
Just as I did once before

God the devil has even taken my emotions
So now it's like I just don't care anymore

So God please help me

James 1:2-7

My brethren,
Count it all joy when you fall into divers temptations;

Knowing this,
That the trying of your faith works patience

But let patience have her perfect work,
That you may be perfect and entire, wanting nothing

If any of you lack wisdom, let him ask of God,
That gives it to all men liberally, and upbraids not;
And it shall be given him

But let him ask in faith,
Nothing wavering for he that wavered
Is like a wave of the sea driven with the wind and tossed

For let not that man think
That he shall receive any thing of the Lord

God I have always heard
That joy would cometh in the morning light

But God how can I smile in the morning
When I think about the lives that were lost last night

God how can I smile
When I think about the children around the world
Whose beds are made out of cold sand

God please enlighten me
Because my tears fall constantly
For the things that I just can't understand

God please give me wisdom
So that I may understand
Everything that I don't

God please bless me with patience
So that I may rightfully earn
Everything that I want

God please hold me up
So that I may not fall
Into temptations hole

God please be my savior
So that I may not backslide
And allow the devil to steal my soul

Please God, I beg of you

And said, I cried by reason of mine affliction unto the Lord,
And he heard me; out of the belly of hell cried I,
And thou heard my voice

For thou had cast me into the deep,
In the midst of the seas; and the floods compassed me about:
All thy billows and thy waves passed over me

Then I said, I am cast out of thy sight;
Yet I will look again toward thy holy temple
The waters compassed me about, even to the soul:
The depth closed me round about,
The weeds were wrapped about my head

I went down to the bottoms of the mountains;
The earth with her bars was about me forever:
Yet hast thou brought me up my life from corruption

O Lord my God

When my soul fainted within me I remembered the Lord:
And my prayer came in unto thee, into thine holy temple

My God I have cried to you
And you have quickly answered me
Because you could hear my pain in my voice

My God I have asked you for knowledge
And you have given it to me
Because you fear that I could make the wrong choice

My God I have prayed for understanding
And you have blessed me
Because you have seen the confusion on my face

My God I have asked you to direct me
And you have lead me
Because you knew I was headed to the wrong place

My God I have asked you for wisdom
And you have taught me
Because I can't teach if I myself am not wise

My God I have asked you for vision
And you have granted it
You have even blessed me to see out of my third eye

My God I have asked a lot of you
Just as you have also asked of me

And my God I can only pray
That I have made you proud being the man
That you have chosen me to be

I write unto you, little children,
Because your sins are forgiven for his name's sake

I write unto you, fathers,
Because you have known him that is from the beginning

I write unto you, young men,
Because you have overcome the wicked one

I written unto you, little children,
Because you have known the Father

I have written to you, fathers,
Because you have known that is from the beginning

I have written unto you, young men,
Because you are strong, and the word of God abides in you,
And you have overcome the wicked ones

Love not the world, neither the things that are in the world
If any man loves the world, the love of the Father is not in him

God just as you have written unto me
I have also taken the time
Just so I can write back unto you

And God I'm sorry if my letters
Have seemed a tad bit harsh
But I write about the pain and poverty
That your young black children often go through

God I use words to paint poetic portraits in watercolor
Using the tears that falls from your children's eyes

God I use words to inspire those with cold hearts
Using me as an example
That there is a sun that shines behind those gray skies

God I use words to open closed minds
Using me as an example
That they can be anything that they want to be

God I use words to motivate the masses
Using the bible as an example
Because it was your words that motivated me

God I use words to write my vows
Using you as an example
Because without vowing to you God
I can never honor any vows to my wife

God I use words to break young yokes
Using Jesus as an example
Because Jesus is our only way to eternal life

Ecclesiastes
7:14-20

In the day of prosperity be joyful,
But in the day of adversity consider:
God also has set the one over against the other,
To the end that man should find nothing after him

All things have I seen in the days of my vanity:
There is a just man that perished in his righteousness,
And there is a wicked man
That prolonged his life in his wickedness

Be not righteous over much; neither make yourself over wise:
Why should you destroy yourself?
Be not over much wicked, neither be foolish:
Why should you die before your time?

It is good that you should take hold of this;
Yea, also from this withdraw not thine hand:
For he that feared God shall come forth to all of them

Wisdom strengthened the wise more than
Ten mighty men, which are in the city
For there is not a just man upon the earth,
That does good, and doesn't sin

God I pray that you understand my decision
If I decide to leave this world
Before it's my time

God I pray that you understand
That I'm tired of all this heartache and pain
And I'm tired of this life of crime

God I pray that you understand
Why I feel that death may be
The only way for me to make it out of the hood

God I pray that you understand
That even though my actions seem evil
My heart's intentions were meant for good

God I pray that you understand
Why my emotions seem to be so cold

God I pray that you understand
Why I've never really cared about growing old

God I pray that you understand
Because it seems as if no one else does
Or maybe they just don't care

God I pray that you understand
Why I feel the way that I feel
And why this is just too much for me to bear

God I just pray that you understand

Mark 11:22-26

And Jesus answering said unto them,
Have faith in God

For verily I say unto you,
That whosoever shall say unto this mountain,
Are thou removed,
And be cast into the sea; and shall not doubt in his heart,
But shall believe that those things
Which he said shall come to pass;
He shall have whatsoever he said

Therefore I say unto you, what things so ever you desire,
When you pray, believe that you will receive them,
And you shall have them

And when you stand praying, forgive,
If you have ought against any:
That your Father also which is in heaven
May forgive you your trespasses

But if you do not forgive,
Neither will your Father, which is in heaven
Forgive your trespasses

God I am planted in your word
Just as a tree by the river's waters
But it seems as if the devil
Has sent his hurricanes to blow me down

God I am as a peasant that became king
But it seems as if the devil
Has sent his soldiers to conquer my crown

God I am as a ship in your ocean
But it seems as if the devil
Has sent his tornadoes to knock me off course

God I am as a fallen angel
But it seems as if the devil
Has taken away my heart's remorse

God I am as a summer's day
But it seems as if the devil
Has sent the moon to eclipse the sun

God I am as a child
But it seems as if the devil
Has broken my spirits
And now I know nothing of fun

God I am as a track star
But it seems as if the devil
Has knocked me off of my feet

God I am as a rose
But it seems as if the devil
Can't stop me from growing through concrete

II John 1:7-12

For many deceivers are entered into the world,
Who confess not that Jesus Christ has come in the flesh
This is a deceiver and an antichrist

Look to yourselves,
That we lose not those things that we have wrought,
But that we receive a full reward

Whosoever transgresses,
And abides not in the doctrine of Christ,
Has not God: He that abides in the doctrine of Christ,
He has both the Father and the Son

If there come any unto you, and bring not this doctrine,
Receive him not into your house, neither bid him God speed:

For he that bides him God speed is partaker of his evil deeds

Having many things to write unto you,
I would not write with paper and ink:
But I trust to come unto you,
And speak face to face, that our joy may be full

God why has my life
Been nothing but a burden
To so many others

God why has my life
Misguided so many of my
Young sisters and brothers

God why has my life
Been filled with
So much heartache and pain

God why has my life
Seemed to be so bright at times
But always gets dampened by rain

God why has my life
Known so much crime

God why has my life
Felt that it will end before its time

God why has my life
Caused my grandma to shed
So many tears

God why has my life
Allowed my sweet dreams
To be invaded by fears

God why has my life
Been this way all my life

Take heed that ye do not your alms before men,
To be seen of them: otherwise ye have no reward
Of your Father which is in heaven

Therefore when thou doest thine alms,
Do not sound a trumpet before thee,
As the hypocrites do in the synagogues and in the streets,
That the may have glory of men
Verily I say unto you, they have their reward

But when thou doest alms,
Let not thy left hand know what thy right hand doeth:

That thine alms may be in secret:
And thy Father which seeth in secret himself
Shall reward the openly

And when thou pray, thou shall not be as the hypocrites are:
For they love to pray standing in the synagogues and in the
corners of the streets, that they may be seen of men
Verily I say unto you, they have their reward

God I found myself screaming fuck the world
Because I heard through the grapevine
That the world said fuck me

God I found myself going all out
Because I heard that the world
Was planning on stopping me
From being who it is that I am destined to be

God I found myself hustling nonstop
Because I heard that the world
Would do all it could to stop my gains

God I found myself not giving a fuck
Because I heard that the world
Was trying to plague my life
With heartaches and pains

God I found myself feeling suicidal
Because I heard that the world
No longer wanted me anymore

God I found myself constantly crying
Because I heard that the world
Would never stop crucifying me
For the mistakes that I've made once before

God I found myself being by myself
Because I heard that in this world
It's just the best way to be

I have not written unto you because you know not the truth,
But because you know it, and that no lie is of the truth
Who is a liar but he that denies the Father and the Son
Whosoever denies the Son; the same hath not the Father:
He that acknowledges the Son hath the Father also

Let that therefore abide in you,
Which you have heard from the beginning
If that which you have heard
From the beginning shall remain in you,
You also shall continue in the Son, and in the Father

And this is the promise
That he has promised us even eternal life
These things have I written unto you
Concerning them that seduce you

But the anointing that you have received of him abides in you,
And you need not that any man teach you:
But as the same anointing teaches you of all things,
And is the truth, And is no lie,
And even as it hath taught you, you shall abide in him

God know that I will never deny you or your son
Because I know that you are the alpha and omega
And Jesus is the truth, the life, and the way

God know that I have studied your doctrine
As it was written to be the truth
So I don't listen to what liars have to say

God know that to the best of my ability
I have tried to abide in your word
But I know that I have no excuse for falling short

God know that I have faith in your word
And I truly believe in my heart
That you won't allow no man of flesh
To misjudge me in life or in court

God know that I have believed in your word
So therefore I truly believe in my heart
That you will never leave me alone

God know that I have found understanding in your word
So therefore I now understand
That it will be okay when I need a shoulder to cry on
And it seems as if everyone is gone

God know that I have found love in your word
So therefore I now find myself
Loving your word

So God thank you for your word

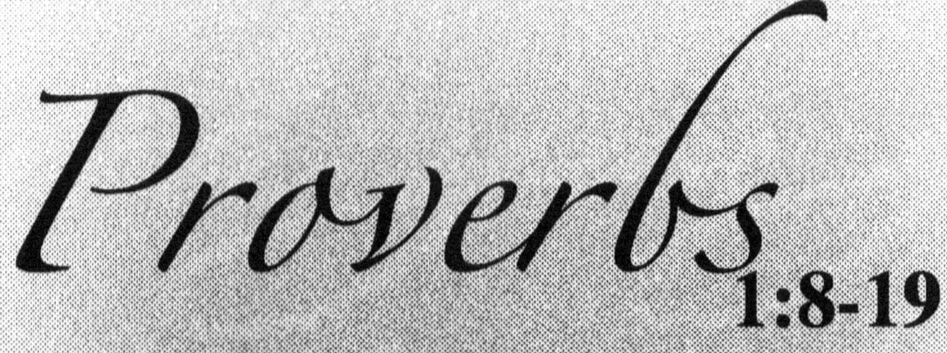

Proverbs 1:8-19

My son, hear the instruction of your father
And do not forsake the law of your mother
For they will be a graceful ornament on your head,
And chains around your neck

My son, if sinners entice you,
Do not consent

My son, walk not thou in the way with them;
Refrain thy foot from their path:

For their feet run to evil,
And make haste to shed blood

Surely in vain the nest is spread in the sight of any bird

And they lay waiting for their own blood;
They lurk secretly for their own lives

So are the ways of every one that is greedy of gain;
Which takes away the life of its owners

God I never thought as a child
That my life would turn out like this

Tears begin to fall from my face
As my mind thinks back
And begins to reminisce

God I was just a young boy that was lost
Searching for nothing but some
Unconditional love and direction

And maybe that's what lured me to the streets
Because at that time in my life
It was only the streets that offered me
Sincere understanding and protection

God I'm sorry for the path that I chose
But the streets seemed to be
The only path that I could see

So God I just followed in the footsteps of those
Who had already beaten down a path just for me

And God I know that I have
Traveled down the wrong path for way too long

So God I pray that you will redirect my life
And put me back on the path that I belong

So instead of my feet running to evil
My feet will now run to you

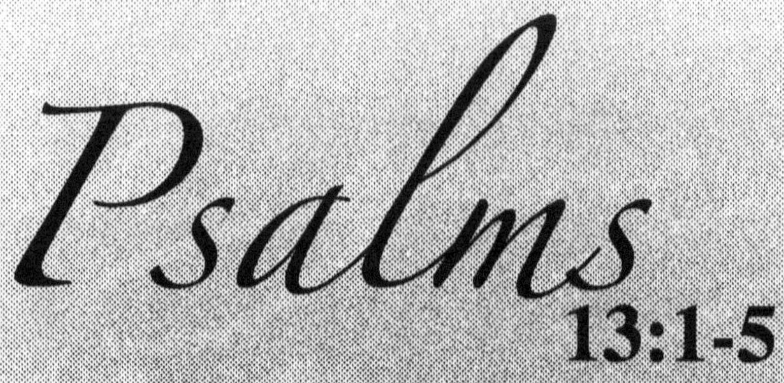

Psalms 13:1-5

How long wilt thou forget me, O Lord?

Forever?

How long wilt thou hide thy face from me?

How long shall I take counsel in my soul?

Having sorrow in my heart daily
How long shall mine enemy be exalted over me?

Consider and hear me,
O Lord my God:
Lighten mine eyes, lest I sleep the sleep of death;

Lest mine enemy say,
I have prevailed against him;
And those that trouble me rejoice when I am moved

But I have trusted in thy mercy;
My heart shall rejoice in thy salvation

God I'm still smiling
Even though my young eyes
Have been filled with so many tears

God I'm still smiling
Even though my sweet dreams
Have been corrupted by fears

God I'm still smiling
Even though my young heart
Has felt so much pain

God I'm still smiling
Even though my young mind
Has almost gone insane

God I'm still smiling
Because I now know
That joy will come in the morning's light

God I'm still smiling
Because I now know
That you'll forgive me for the wrong
That I may have done last night

God I'm still smiling
Because I now know
That you will never give me
More than I can bear

God I'm still smiling
Because I now know
That no matter what I may go through
You will always be right there

Romans
12:8-13

He that exhorts, on exhortation:
He that gives, let him do it with simplicity;

He that rules, with diligence;
He that shows mercy, with cheerfulness

Let love be without dissimulation
Abhor that which is evil; cleave to that which is good

Be kindly affectionate one to another with brotherly love;
In honor preferring on another;

Not slothful in business; fervent in spirit; serving the Lord;

Rejoicing in hope; patient in tribulation;
Continuing instant in prayer;

Distributing to the necessity of saints;
Given to hospitality

God the Bible teaches me
That to whom much is given
Much is required of them to give

God the Bible also teaches me
That in order for me to truly prosper in life
Living humbly is the only way that I can live

God the Bible teaches me
That when prayers go up
Blessings will shower back down

God the Bible also teaches me
That those who voted that you be king
May be the same people
That are plotting to steal your crown

God the Bible teaches me
That when I became a man
I had to put away all of my childish ways

God the Bible also teaches me
That I should love even my enemies
Because only a pure heart
Can promise me a life with eternal days

God the Bible teaches me
That I should live my life accordingly
Because the bible is the law of the land

God the Bible also teaches me
That no matter what
You will never let go of my hand

Ephesians

4:26-32

Be you angry, and sin not:
Let not the sun go down upon your wrath:
Neither give place to the devil

Let him that stole, steal no more:
But rather let him labor, working with his hands
The thing, which is good,
That he may have to give to him that needed

Let no corrupt communication proceed out of your mouth,
But that which is good to the use of edifying,
That it may minister grace unto the hearers
And grieve not the Holy Spirit of God,
Whereby you are sealed unto the day of redemption

Let all bitterness, and wrath,
And anger, and clamor, and evil speaking,
Be put away from you, with all malice:

And be kind to one another,
Tenderhearted, forgiving one another,
Even as God for Christ's sake hath forgiven you

God I ask that you cover me with your blood
Before these niggas in these streets cover me with my own
Please shine your light on my life
Before these niggas light up my life by busting their chrome

God I'm in a war right now
And it seems as if they want me dead or alive
God I ask that you give me the strength to carry on
Because in a war such as this, only the strong will survive

And God I know what goes around comes around
Just as if you live by the gun, you'll probably die by the gun
So therefore I'll probably drown in my own pool of blood
Unless you depart the red sea,
So that I may have somewhere to run

God give me the power to stop these bullets
And show me that I really am the one
And give me the courage to fight against these demons
Until my last days on this earth are done

God hold me up with your right hand
So that I may overcome all the evils of this earth
And God please protect me from all these demons
That have been trying to destroy me since my birth

God help me win this war between good and evil
Because I'm losing the battle between spirit and flesh
But please don't cast me away just yet
Because my heart is built with your blood and righteousness

POETIC PRAYERS

OF A FALLEN ANGEL

Isaiah 51:4-6

Hearken unto me, my people; and give ear unto me,
O my nation: for a law shall proceed from me,
And I will make my judgment to rest for a light of the people

My righteousness is near; my salvation is gone forth,
And mine arms shall judge the people;
The isles shall wait upon me,
And on mine arm shall they trust

Lift up your eyes to the heavens,
And look upon the earth beneath:
For the heavens shall vanish away like smoke,
And the earth shall wax old like a garment,
And they that dwell therein shall die in like manner:
But my salvation shall be forever,
And my righteousness shall not be abolished

Hearken unto me, you that know righteousness,
The people in whose heart is my law; fear ye not the reproach
Of men, neither be ye afraid of their reviling

For the moth shall eat them up like a garment,
And the worm shall eat them like wool;
But my righteousness shall be forever,
And my salvation from generation to generation

Have you ever really thought about what may happen on Judgment Day? Sometimes I often wonder what questions God may ask and how will he Judge his people. I wonder if God will be judging us on a curved scale, or will he let nothing slide. If you really think about it, we all have backslide in one way or another, so will God judge us on our downfalls or will he judge us on our hearts. Many of us sin purposely knowing that we are going against God's will, but the Bible teaches us that if we repent and ask God for forgiveness then he will cast our sins out into the sea of forgiveness. That doesn't mean that it's okay to sin, and you can sin at will, but it does show us that our God is a very compassionate and forgiving God.

I myself have made a lot of mistakes in life, and I pray that God forgives me for all of my sins, but I also know that just as I've broken laws of the land and had to suffer the consequences, I must also reap what I sow for breaking Gods law. I believe that continuously praying to God for forgiveness is just as the little boy who constantly cried wolf. Not saying that God will ignore your cry, but it may become old to him especially if you keep going back out into the world and doing the same old sins. Even though I truly believe in the power of prayer, I also believe that we as a people also must make a great contribution to God concerning our prayers. I believe that we can wait on God to find us or bless us all we want, but until we make the effort to search for God so we can truly benefit from our blessings, we are praying in vain.

How do you think God will judge you at the gates of heaven? Do you think that you will have the answers that he will be looking for, or do you think your name will already be written in the stone tablets? If God only asked you one question, do you think that you would know the correct answer? What if God asked you do you truly believe in him and that Jesus died on the cross for all of our sins, could you undoubtedly say yes?

Proverbs
1:24-31

Because I have called, and you refused;
I have stretched out my hand, and no man regarded;

Because you have disdained
All my counsel and would none of my reproof:

I also will laugh at your calamity;
I will mock when distress and anguish cometh upon you

Then shall they call upon me, but I will not answer;
They shall seek me early, but they shall not find me:

For that they hated knowledge,
And did not choose the fear of the Lord:

They would none of my counsel:
They despised all my reproof

Therefore shall they eat of the fruit of their own way,
And be filled with their own devices

Do you suppose that some of our trials and tribulations that we all go through is just Gods way of sometimes slapping us in the face. Imagine if you were God and it seemed as if your children never listened to you and seemed to rebel on your every word, just as many children of the world do today. How many times have you just wanted to snatch that child by the neck just to get their undivided attention, or slap them in the face to send a message? I have often wondered if God sometimes allow things to happen to us as a wake up call or if he punishes us for being disobedient children.

Think about how many times you said, God if you only get me through this or that then I'll never do it again, and as soon as God helps you get out of the situation at hand, you go back and put yourself into the same hole. The Bible teaches us that our God is a forgiving God, but don't you think he gets tired of hearing that same old story, wouldn't you get tired of hearing it? I believe that God sometimes allows us to suffer just so we can learn a lesson. Do you think that God gets a kick out of seeing his children suffer, or maybe it's like my grandmother always told me before she would beat me; baby it's gonna hurt me more than it hurts you, but it's for your own good.

Imagine you were God, would you not feel the need to laugh and say, I told you so every now and then. Would you not find it amusing playing hide and seek with some of your most faithful sinners, because if you really think about it, we play hide and seek with God all the time. It's like he seeks after us and we run and hide from him, but as soon as we need him, we tend to beg and cry wondering why has our God forsaken us. Have you ever thought about how God must feel when we turn our backs on him, but we always expect for him to be there for us. Think about that friend or family member that's never around until they need something, how does that make you feel?

Unto thee, O Lord, do I lift up my soul

O my God, I trust in thee, let me not be ashamed,
Let not mine enemies' triumph over me

Yea, let none that wait on thee be ashamed:
Let them be ashamed which transgress without cause

Show me thy ways, O Lord; teach me thy paths

Lead me in thy truth, and teach me:
For thou art the God of my salvation;
On thee do I wait all the day

Remember, O Lord,
Thy tender mercies and thy loving kindnesses;
For they have been ever of old

Remember not the sins of my youth,
Nor my transgressions: according to thy mercy
Remember thou me for thy goodness sake, O Lord

I remember when I started The Rally open mic night in Raleigh, NC at a little coffee house for the youth to come out an express themselves through whatever medium of their choice. Some would sing, some would recite poetry, and some would even play musical instruments such as guitars. It seemed as if every week it would be a totally different crowd that would come through the door. The coolest thing about The Rally to me was that not only was it multiracial, and multicultural, but the young people had no problem expressing their love for God.

I myself have always based my poems on the struggles of life and the streets with a spiritual background that many considered as thug prayers. I never really thought of what I wrote to be considered as thug prayers, but more as prayers from the heart of a person who has seen what's on both sides of the fence. Someone once told me that my writing would serve as a ministry to the youth, and if I would lead him or her in the right direction, they would follow. So that's why I make it my mission to write or recite what I feel God has chosen for me to minister. Not saying I'm the first, but I can definitely see my young flock following in my footsteps.

It does my heart good to see a young person speak so passionately about their love for God and not at all be ashamed. The Bible teaches us that the tongue is mightier than the mightiest fist, because life and death lies within the tongue. So instead of always killing each other with negativity, we should begin uplifting each other with positive words and encouragement. I believe that God has placed a special ministry or testimony in each on of us that he feels will help someone else, but it doesn't do the world any good if you're ashamed to speak about Gods glory just because of what your peers may think, because it's them that may need to hear it the most.

Ecclesiastes
8:8-12

There is no man
That has power over the spirit to retain the spirit;
Neither does he have the power in the day of death;
And there is no discharge in that war;
Neither shall wickedness deliver those that are given to it

All this have I seen, and applied my heart unto
Every work that is done under the sun:
There is a time where no man rules over another to his own hur

And so I saw the wicked buried,
Who had come and gone from the place of the holy,
And they were forgotten in the city where they had so done:
This is also vanity

Because sentence against an evil work is not executed speedily,
Therefore the heart of the sons of men
Is fully set in them to do evil

Though a sinner do evil a hundred times,
And his days be prolonged,
Yet surely I know that it shall be well with those that fear God,
Which fear before him

A friend of mine named Tim Jackson wrote a poem entitled "How many of my people are willing to die for God", and it seemed the more I heard that poem, the deeper that question became. When I think back to what happen on September 11, 2001, and all that has transpired after that, I began to wonder. I wondered if God would come back right now and asked us to follow him into the valley of death, how many of us would actually be willing to follow God knowing that were going to die.

Some may call them suicide bombers, but I prefer to call them sacrificial spiritual soldiers. Take a moment and think about it, even Jesus was hated by the people, and was sacrificed up on the cross. Did he not choose to give his life in the name of God believing that God would bless him with everlasting life after death? Don't you think that Jesus trusted that God would bring him back from the dead, just as many of Iraq's people still believe today? Our President George Bush claimed it to be a terrorist attack on America, but no one ever mentioned how we have terrorized Iraq for years for their Oil. Iraqis says it's a Holy War to protect their Holy Land, and America says it's a War on Terrorism, but who's the real terrorist in this matter. How would you feel if someone invaded your house and then told you how you should live in the house that your grandfather built with his own hands? The sad thing about it is, that analogy probably comes nowhere close to how the Iraqis feel about America.

I understand that the President is a powerful man and also has a lot of responsibilities that lies on his shoulders to govern his people. But I don't believe that the President have the power to sacrifice soldiers at war for his own personal vendetta. What kind of leader sends his soldiers to war just before he goes to bed, to me that's not a leader, that's a supervisor. The Bible teaches me that God said Vengeance is Mine, I will repay.

Romans
12:17-21

Recompense to no man evil for evil.
Provide things hones in the sight of all men

If it be possible, as much as lies in you,
Live peaceably with all men

Dearly beloved, avenge not yourselves,
But rather give place unto wrath:
For it is written, vengeance is mine;
I will repay, said the Lord

Therefore if thine enemy hungers, feed him;
If he thirsts, give him drink;
For in so doing thou shalt heap coals of fire on his head

Be not overcome of evil,
But overcome evil with good

Kill or be killed seems to the mentality of the youth today. It's easier said than done to turn the other cheek, just as it's easier said than done to have no thought of revenge against someone that has harmed you in any way. Even though it has been written in the word of God that vengeance is his, most people take the law in their own hands, just as the law takes the law of God in their own hands. Don't get me wrong because I feel that the law of the land should enforce rules of the world, but I feel that taking some ones life is crossing over into Gods territory.

The bible teaches us that we should do unto others, as we would want them to do unto us, and maybe that's why many feel that they should do unto others as others have done unto them. But if you really think about it, it was God who said that the law of the land should be enforced by an eye for an eye and a tooth for a tooth.

Deuteronomy 19:15-21 reads; One witness shall not rise against a man concerning any iniquity or any sin that he commits; by the mouth of two or three witnesses the matter shall be established. If a false witness rises against any man to testify against him in wrongdoing, then both men in the controversy shall stand before the Lord, before the priests and the judges who serve in those days. And the judges shall make careful inquiry, and indeed, if the witness is a false witness, who has testified falsely against his brother, then you shall do to him as ha thought to have done to his brother; so you shall put away the evil from among you (does this mean kill those that want to see you dead). And those who remain shall hear and fear, and hereafter they shall not again commit such evil among you. Your eye shall not pity: life shall be for life, eye for eye, tooth for tooth, hand for hand, and foot for foot. Please read this scripture for yourself so that you may have a better understanding.

Titus 1:7-16

For a bishop must be blameless, as the steward of God;
Not self-willed, not soon angry, not given to wine,
No striker, not given to filthy lucre;

But a lover of hospitality,
A lover of good men, sober, just, holy, temperate;

Holding fast the faithful word as he hath been taught,
That he may be able by sound doctrine
Both to exhort and to convince the gainsayers

For there are many unruly and vain talkers and deceivers,
Especially they of the circumcision:

Whose mouths must be stopped,
Who subvert whole houses,
Teaching things which they ought not,
For filthy lucre's sake

They profess that they know God;
But in works they deny him, being abominable,
And disobedient, and unto every good work reprobate

Have you ever really thought about how hard it must be to be a bishop? Can you imagine having not only Gods eyes on you around the clock, but also the eyes of the world? My girl Tina a.k.a. Woman Storm once asked a question in one of her poems which said, where does the sun go for light. Imagine if you had to put yourself last on the priority list, which means that you would have to cater to everyone else needs before you could even think about yourself. I can imagine that must a difficult task, especially when you not only have to put friends and family before yourself, but also so those who may have caused harm to you in the past and those that some may consider your enemy.

I truly believe that God sent Jesus to this world to be a living example or shall I say a spiritual role model for the people of the world to use as guide to pattern their lives after. As a matter of fact, that goes for anyone in a spiritual leadership position, no matter if you're a bishop, pastor, evangelist, or even just a preacher, God has given you the responsibility to lead his people by not only his words, but also by example. It's just as the scripture says, to whom much is given, much is required.

Just imagine how you would feel if you found out that the man or woman you looked up to as a spiritual role model was not who they portrayed themselves to be. What if you found out that they were a homosexual or a lesbian, I know I myself would be hurt to find out that the man that I've always put on a pedestal in my life, was not really even a man. It's an old saying that says that you should practice what you preach, and I truly believe that with all my heart. How can I tell a child not to smoke if every time that child sees me I'm smoking more than a chimney on Christmas day. Should I really expect that child to listen to me or even respect me if I don't practice what I preach, would you?

Ezekiel 18:30-32

I will judge you, O house of Israel,
Every one according to his ways,
Said the Lord God

Repent, and turn yourselves from all your transgressions;
So iniquity shall not be your ruin

Cast away from all your transgressions,
Whereby you have transgressed;

And make you a new heart and a new spirit:
For why will you die, O house of Israel?

For I have no pleasure in the death of him that dies,
Said the Lord God:
Wherefore turn yourselves, and you shall live

The bible teaches us that in order for one to be born again, one must die. When I got saved, I worried if some of the old me continued to live on within my heart, even though I have started a new life. I later on learned that nothing will completely change overnight, but the most important thing that I found that had changed was my heart. A lot of the things that my young flesh use to desire was no longer desired by the new me. I had also learned that for the rest of my life, I will struggle daily trying to walk in the light of God, but as long as you keep taking steps to get closer to God, the God will take two steps to your one step to get closer to you. Even when you may backslide, God will continue walking towards you, but the more you backslide the longer it will take you to get to him.

I remember when I was living a life of crime; I always felt the need to look over my shoulder. It seemed that every police in the world always had it out for me, it seemed as if they always had their eyes on me, but I later on learned in life that I was just paranoid. When I put that life behind me and started my new life, I felt so much peaceful, and never once did I feel that need to look over my shoulder to see if some one was plotting on me. It's like I began to understand all of the heartaches and pain that I've encountered in life. So now I thank God for a lesson learned.

I've learned that I have the opportunity to dig my own grave, just as I have the opportunity to live forever in heaven. I also had the opportunity to live forever in hell if I would have continued to rebel against Gods will. It's a beautiful thing that God loves us enough to forgive us for all of our sins and transgressions so we can have a second chance for heaven.

Psalms 25:8-13

Good and upright is the Lord:
Therefore will he teach sinners in the way?

The meek will he guide in judgment,
And the meek will he teach his way

All the paths of the Lord are mercy and truth
Unto such as keep his covenant and his testimonies

For thy name's sake; O Lord,
Pardon mine iniquity; for it is great

What man is he that fears the Lord?
Him shall he teach in the way that he shall choose

His soul shall dwell at ease;
And his see shall inherit the earth

Have you ever thought about why it seems as if God picks what seems to be the most unrighteous people in the world to become leaders to his people. If you take a look back into time, the most powerful leaders were once in their life prisoners. Even John the Baptist was once a prisoner, as a matter of fact, John even died on what is now called death row. Maybe what seems to be unrighteous in the human eye isn't on Gods eye. Maybe we all go through a period of trials and tribulations as a part of Gods plan for us. I guess sometimes we just don't realize that.

I think about the two leaders that have influenced my life, which happens to be Malcolm X, and Tupac Shakur. Both were ex-cons, but both also had an unbelievable way with words to the hearts and minds of the people. Maybe God picks the people he knows has the ability to reach the people that he wants to reach. Maybe that's why he places some people in the church behind the pulpit, and others such as Tupac in the streets, and someone such as Malcolm to be placed in the public eye for both the church and the streets. No matter were God places a person, he has already prepared them. God has already taught them and molded them to teach his people the way that he wants them to be taught.

I have often wondered what is Gods plan for me. I truly believe in my heart that my whole life has been nothing but basic training to become one of Gods spiritual soldiers. I now believe that God has chosen me to reach his people through my poetry and testimonies. What better person could lead you from somewhere, than somebody that has already been there? Now I understand that all of my trials and tribulations has been nothing but God testing my faith. I just pray that I have passed the test.

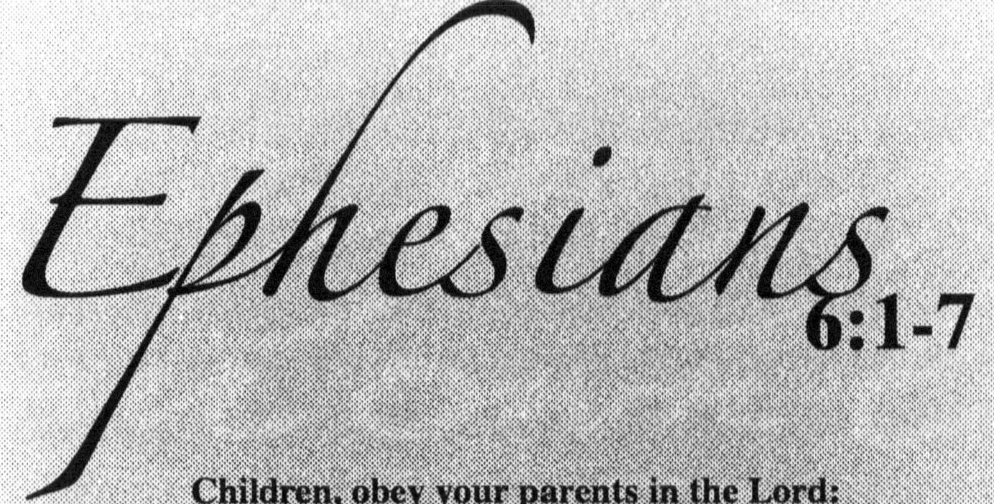

Children, obey your parents in the Lord:
For this is right

Honor your father and mother;
Which is the first commandment with promise;

That it may be well with thee,
And you may live long on the earth

And, you fathers, provoke not your children to wrath:
But bring them up in the nurture and admonition of the Lord

Servants, be obedient to them that are your masters
According to the flesh, with fear and trembling,
In singleness of your heart, as unto Christ;

Not with eye service, as men pleasers;
But as the servants of Christ,
Doing the will of God form the heart;

With good will doing service, as to the Lord, and not to men

The bible teaches us that we should honor and obey our mothers and fathers, but it seems easier said than done, especially in a day and time such as now. Many of the children today may not even know their mothers or fathers, I know for as myself, I was raised and reared by my grandmother every since I could remember, so therefore, I have no childhood bond with either my mother or father. Now don't get me wrong because I love both my mother and father, but at the same time it's kind of hard for me to honor someone that I feel never really honored me, especially with me being their child. The bible also teaches us that fathers should not provoke their children to wrath, well the bible only says fathers, but I feel that it should say parents should not provoke your children to wrath. I have often wondered that if a child were provoked to rebel from his or her parents, would their actions be justified in the eyes of God. Maybe God understands the child's actions since he already knows the situation that the child is in. On the other hand, maybe God expects us even as children to turn the other cheek, and honor and obey thy mother and father anyway.

The bible also teaches us that servants should be obedient to their masters, now I'm still praying that God gives me insight so that I may understand exactly what this means. Some of you may agree with me when I say, being a young black man in America, the statement that servants should be obedient to their masters doesn't sit well with my soul. On top of that, the scripture also states that according to flesh, not according to the spirit, but according to the flesh with fear and trembling. God please forgive me when I say this, but all I can see in my mind when I read this is a slave master telling his slave to plow the field as he stands there with his wipe in hand or pointing at the tree that he will hang the slave from if the slave doesn't do as he says. So if anyone has a meaning that they can share with me on this scripture, please feel free to email me at sean@seaningram.com. Because I can use all the help I can get in this spiritual journey.

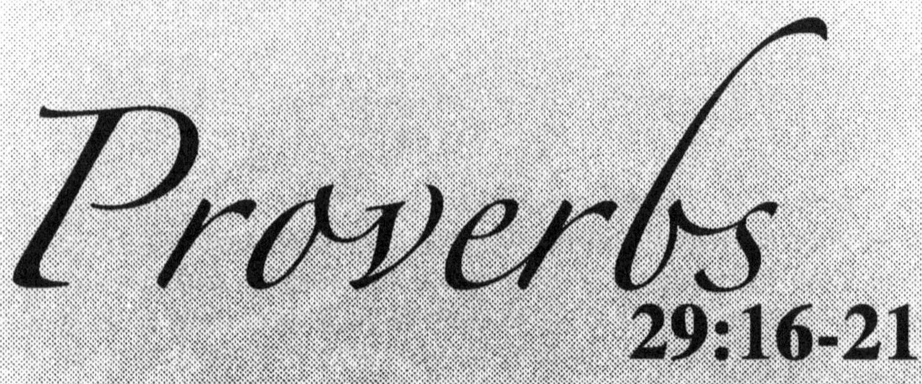

Proverbs

29:16-21

When the wicked are multiplied, transgression increases:
But the righteous shall see their fall

Correct thy son, and he shall give thee rest;
Yea, he shall give delight unto thy soul

Where there is no vision, the people perish:
But he that keeps the law, happy is he

A servant will not be corrected by words:
For though he understand he will not answer

Sees thou a man that is hast in his words
There is more hope of a fool than of him

He that delicately brings up his servant from a child
Shall have him become his son at the length

I pray that if I ever have a son, I can lead him in the right direction so he won't have to travel the same unbeaten paths as I did. I pray that I can break the cycle that my dad and granddad have cursed me with. My granddaddy lived a life of crime, just as my daddy has also lived a life of crime, and wouldn't you know that I also found myself living a life of crime, so I pray that my son don't find himself walking in our shoes.

I have never learned to be a father, so I guess I'll just do the opposite of my dad, and everything will be okay. Maybe if I had a real male role model in my life as a child, I wouldn't have brought so much pain in my grandmothers' life. Regardless if I have a son or a daughter, I plan on raising them with love and spiritual guidance so they may not have to go through the same things that I have been through in life. I hope that my children bring more joy into my life, rather than the pain that I saw my grandmothers children bring into hers. I pray that I can stop this chain reaction with my children; I pray that I can show them the vision, so that they may not perish as I did. All I really want for my kids is a better life than I had.

I'm so glad that God has changed my life before he allowed me to have children. Maybe my dad was never a father to me, because his dad was never a father to him, so therefore he never learned to be a father. Maybe I am the way I am because my dad taught me to survive by any means necessary, and maybe that's all he knew to teach me because that was all his dad had taught him. Can you see how life works, and how this chain reaction effects everyone that's a link on this chain. Well I plan to break this chain reaction cycle, even if it means that I have to break the chain.

Wherefore the Lord said,
For as much as this people

Draw near me with their mouth,
And with their lips do honor me,

But have removed their heart far from me,
And their fear toward me
Is taught by the precept of men:

Therefore, behold,

I will proceed to do a marvelous work among this people,
Even a marvelous work and a wonder:

For the wisdom of their wise men shall perish,
And the understanding of their prudent men shall be hid

God said that if I would draw near to him with my mouth, and honor him with my lips, he would proceed to do marvelous works with me. Not only will he do marvelous with me, but he will also bless me to the point that may make others even wonder, not only others, but even I myself may not be able to understand why God has blessed me so. I truly am a living witness of Gods marvelous works, but it took me years to see how God has blessed me with the ability to reach and touch people through my poetry. Every one has a special gift or talent that God has blessed you with, and through that special gift or talent is your personal way to praise God. Maybe that's why I have been so blessed, because every word that I write is to honor God. Every time I step on a stage to recite poetry, my mission is to honor God and to spread the word that he has given to me. Sometimes I even find myself redirecting my poems, I guess God sees someone in the crowed that needs to hear something that I wasn't planning on saying. That just goes to show how God works through me, because I am only a vessel for his words, because God speaks through me.

I have learned in life that no matter what your special gift or talent is, if you do it to the glory of God, you will prosper from it more than you could ever imagine. It seems the more I honor God in my works, the more he blesses me financially and promotionally. I remember when my first book was released, it seemed as if I would run myself to death trying to reach the people, but now that I have grown so much spiritually, it seems that the people are doing all they can to reach me. I've learned that everyone is searching for truth and righteousness, and it seems as if everyone is looking for a physical leader that they can look up too. I just pray that I can lead the people that look up to me in the right direction, but since I'm walking towards God now, I feel that we will be alright. And know that I will never forsake you, because God has never once forsaken me.

Love not the world,
Neither the things that are in the world

If any man loves the world,
The love of the Father is not in him

For all that is in the world,

The lust of the flesh,
And the lust of the eyes,
And the pride of life,
Is not of the Father but of the world

And the world passed away,
And the lust thereof:
But he that doeth the will of God abides forever

So many people go to hell for not obeying this very
scripture. I myself have struggled my whole life with loving the
things of the world, and lets not even talk about lusting the flesh,
and if it's one thing attracts me most to a beautiful women is her
beautiful eyes. I now know that the devil has attacked me in my
weakest areas, and maybe that's why God has allowed for me to
be incarcerated. I guess it's like fasting, because now I can want
for none of that. Maybe God feels that if I learn to go without
in prison, then maybe when I 'm released I can continue to have
the strength to go without. I hope God is right, because as of this
point, lust is my biggest downfall, and how can I let a women that
probably don't even really care about me stop me from going to
heaven to be with God who I know loves me unconditionally.

The bible teaches us that money is the root to all evil, but
I feel that it's the love of money that brings evil. The love of
money brings greed, and where there is greed, there is a need to
have by any means necessary. Criminals don't do what they do
just because they think it's cute or fun, they do it because they
feel that they have to have the money. When greed takes over
the mind, that when one truly becomes criminal minded. In their
mind, they can never have enough money, and that's why you
have young drug dealers going all out to get that money, because
the more money you have, the more problems you will have, and
the more problems you have, the more money you will need.

A lot of our kids have an all or nothing mentality, especially
when they have come from having nothing. And a lot of the
people that seems to have made it in life has the mentality that
they will do whatever it take not to go back to where they came
from, which is probably poverty. So really it's the love of money
that brings greed which brings evil.

In thee, O Lord, so I put my trust;
Let me never be ashamed:
Deliver me in thy righteousness

Bow down thine ear to me;
Deliver me speedily: be thou my strong rock,
For an house of defense to save me

For thou art my rock and my fortress;
Therefore for thy name's sake lead me, and guide me

Pull me out of the net that they have laid secretly for me:
For thou art my strength

Into thine hand I commit my spirit:
Thou hast redeemed me, O Lord God of truth

I have whole-heartedly put my love and trust in God. I have mentally stepped out of myself and turned my life over to him, because I know that he will make better decisions for me than I ever have for myself. I have mentally given God full control to guide me in whatever direction he feels that would be of benefit to myself, and to his kingdom. In my past years, I've done all I know to do to prosper in life whether it was right or wrong, and it seemed as if nothing worked. I later on learned in life that I would never prosper in life without God being the head of my life. I have vowed to God that whenever I have to opportunity to speak to the masses, I will truth from my heart, and I will never be ashamed to speak about the glory of God.

God has promised me that as long as I continue to speak for him, he continue to protect me form all of the people that may throw stones at me. God has already told me that it's not going to be an easy journey, but he will give me the strength to stand strong even at my weakest moments, and he will shield me from those that will stand up against me for speaking the truth. Knowing that God is in my corner, whom shall I fear, and if God is for me, then who even in hell can be against me.

God has even blessed with foresight so that I may see ahead of time those situations that I'll be walking in. God has already informed me about the traps that people will set for me, but God has given me the vision to walk with my eyes closed in a minefield and not step on one mine. God has even placed me up on a rock, so those that want to pull me down in life can't touch me. I pray that God continues to use me as he sees fit. I pray that my words will continue to uplift my people and also uplift the name of God. I also pray that God will continue to guide me so I can lead those that follow me in the right direction mentally and spiritually.

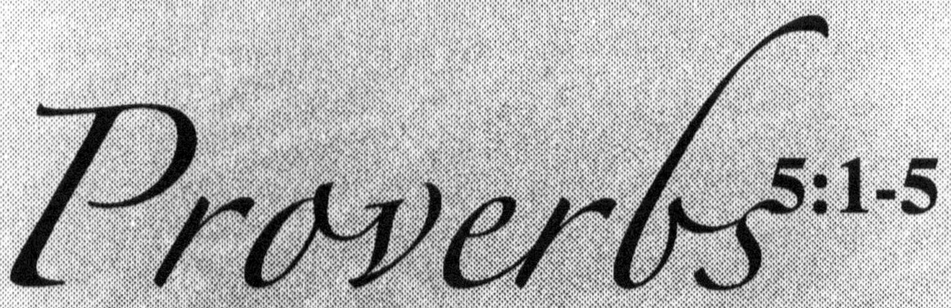

My son,
Attend unto my wisdom,
And bow thine ear to my understanding:

That thou mayest regard discretion,
And that thy lips may keep knowledge

For the lips of a strange woman drop as a honeycomb,
And her mouth is smoother than oil:

But her end is better as wormwood,
Sharp as a two-edged sword

Her feet go down to death; her steps take hold on hell

After reading this scripture, I found myself being afraid of every beautiful woman that I met. It was always in the back of my mind that she was sent by the devil to attract me and then attack me. I have always known that women have been my biggest downfall in life, so what better way for the devil to attack me than sending a beautiful, smooth talking woman my way. It's a good thing that God has blessed me with the ability to look into some ones eyes and see right into their soul, because that allows me to see the good or bad in some one from the beginning. I know as for myself, I have always been attracted more to a certain type of women than I have another, but it seems that every time I meet a women that fits that type, we can't seem to get along for very long, maybe that's God way of telling me that she's no good for me and that's just part of the devils delusion.

During my spiritual growth, not only have I grown to believe in God, but I have also grown to believe in the devil. If you have ever studied the bible, you can see how the devil sends temptation to us to test our love for God. And if you really think about it, God allows the devil to test us, I guess he also wants to know if you will fall into the temptations of this world. God has allowed the devil to test his people since the beginning of time, and when I say his people, I mean some of his closes people such as Eve, Job, and even Jesus himself. If you have ever read the story of Job, you will see what lengths the devil will go to get you turn from God. Trust me, if the devil can't get you to come to hell his way, then he will surly give you hell on earth if you're trying to live Gods way. So therefore I thank God for my wisdom and understanding, and I pray that I will never allow one of the devils beautiful woman to convince me to follow her, because God has already told me that her feet will lead me to death and straight to hell.

Hearken unto me,

You that know righteousness,
The people in whose heart is my law;

Fear ye not the reproach of Men,
Neither be ye afraid of their reviling

For the moth shall eat them up like a garment,
And the worm shall eat them like wool;

But my righteousness shall be forever,
And my salvation from generation to generation

My mission in life is to live forever, first of all I want to live forever in the kingdom of God, and secondly I want to live forever through my poetry by continuing to stay in the hearts and minds of those I will leave behind from generation to generation. The bible has taught me that the only way I can accomplish this mission is for me to live righteously. But I must admit that it's an everyday struggle for me. Please don't get me wrong, because I do have love in my heart and a want to do what's righteous, but sometimes pain and anger clouds my judgment, which sometimes causes me to do wrong and make poor decisions.

Sometimes I wish that I would have had more positive male role models in my life, then maybe my life wouldn't have turned out the way that it did. That's why I have dedicated my life to be a positive male role model for those that may look towards me for guidance and inspiration. Even though the responsibility seems to put the weight of the world on my shoulders, I feel very blessed and fortunate that God would even appoint me to be in this position. Must I must admit that I do sometimes worry about my beliefs, I'm not worried about my belief in God, but my beliefs and views of the world. I pray that God teaches me the truth so I won't lead his people with an unrighteous heart. Because I know that the blind can not lead the blind, and I can't lead anyone anywhere if I don't know the direction.

I pray that God continues to speak to my heart so that I may know the words to speak to others, I pray that allows me to have a receptive ear to the words that he has spoken to me. I pray that God forgives me for all of my sins and all of my unrighteous thoughts and feelings. I also pray that you forgive me for any unrighteous things that I may have said or written, but please remember I write from the heart, so I ask that you will pray for me that I will continue to grow in the Lord.

James
1:13-17

Let no man say when he is tempted,
I am tempted of God:
For God cannot be tempted with evil,
Neither tempted he any man:

But every man is tempted,
When he is drawn away of his own lust, and enticed

Then when lust hath conceived,
It brings forth sin:
And sin, when it is finished,
Brings forth death

Do not err, my beloved brethren

Every good gift and every perfect gift is from above,
And cometh down from the Father of lights,
With whom is no variableness, neither shadow of turning

The temptations of the world seem to be every ones downfall in life. I have always heard that curiosity is what killed the cat, and it seems to be what will also kill man. Earlier on in this book, I spoke about mans downfall to the temptation of the flesh. If you have studied the bible you may have noticed that the devil uses temptation to destroy us more than he uses sickness or death. Even in the beginning of time, the devil tempted Eve to eat fruit from the tree that was in the mist of the garden. The devil has always been able to such a cunning character even when he's in the form of a serpent. The devils ability to deceive you is like no other, and maybe that's why he come in the form of something that he knows will attract you from a far. Not only does he attract you by his physical appearance, but also the words that will come out of his mouth will be smooth and convincing.

The bible teaches us how the serpent approached Eve with what seemed to be small talk saying, did God tell you that you couldn't eat any fruit. And then Eve replied, No, we can eat the fruit that came from the trees in the garden, but we don't suppose to eat from the tree that's in the mist of the garden because if we do than we would surely die. And this is were the devils cunningness comes in, the devil replied to Eve saying, you won't die, as a matter of fact God doesn't want you to eat that fruit because he knows that you eyes will be opened and you will become as God. I can just hear Eve now saying as a woman would, Oh Yeah, well I'll show him, and wouldn't you believe she ate fruit from the tree. Not only did Eve eat the fruit, but also being the woman that she was, she wasn't planning going down by herself, so therefore she convinced Adam to eat some of the apple, so now we all have to pay for their mistakes. So ladies please don't get mad at us men in the labor room, because it ain't our fault that labor is painful, you can blame that one on your girl Eve.

He that has to be rich hath an evil eye,
And considers not tat poverty shall come upon him

He that rebukes a man afterwards shall find more favor
Than he that flatters with the tongue

Whosoever robes his father or his mother
And said, it is no transgression;
The same is the companion of a destroyer

He that is of a proud heart stirs up strife;
But he that puts his trust in the Lord shall be made fat

He that trusts in his own heart is a fool:
But whosoever walks wisely, he shall be delivered

He that gives unto the poor shall not lack:
But he that hides his eyes shall have many a curse

I have learned in life that one must be willing to give unselfishly, in order to receive. The scripture reads; He that gives unto the poor man shall not lack, but he that has to be rich has an evil eye. In the past few years, I found myself subconsciously giving to people with no expectations in return, and honestly, I didn't even realize that I was doing it until a friend of mine brought it to my attention. I began the Sean Ingram Foundation for that very reason, because I have always believed that God would bless me for sharing the fruits of my labor with those who are less fortunate. Please don't misunderstand me, because I don't have a lot to share financially, but I do have ways to provide for those who may go without. Being that the Sean Ingram Foundation is an non-profit organization, we can normally get other businesses to sponsor us on different events. Sponsors mean a great deal, especially when it comes to feeding the homeless.

Many people may feel that I only do these things for the promotional aspect of it, but I do these things because I know first hand how it feels to go without, and besides that, I know in my heart that it's the right thing to do and God will bless for doing good deeds unto his people. I have never really been homeless, but I have slept in my car more nights than I would have liked too, and I have also gone to bed hungry more nights than I would like to remember. But I really do it because God told me too.

Some may criticize me for not paying a lot in tithes, and don't get me wrong because I feel that every one should pay tithes, but I just don't believe that the only way can you pay tithes to God is in the church. I believe that instead of paying alot of money to the church for tithes, we should give to the community and the schools, at least feed the ones in need. So instead of paying money that I really can't afford to pay in tithes, I give to the community as much as I possibly can. I just pray that God understands.

Psalms 31:9-15

Have mercy upon me, O Lord, for I am in trouble:
Mine eye is consumed with grief, yea, my soul and my belly

For my life is spent with grief, and my years with sighing:
My strength failed because of mine iniquity,
And my bones are consumed

I was a reproach among all mine enemies,
But especially among my neighbors,
And a fear to mine acquaintance:
They that did see me without fled from me

I am forgotten as a dead man out of mind:
I am like a broken vessel

For I have heard the slander of many:
Fear was on every side:
While they took counsel together against me,
They devised to take away my life

But I trusted in thee, O Lord: I said, Thou art my God

My times are in thy hand:
Deliver me from the hand of mine enemies,
And from them that persecute me

I truly thank God for the unconditional love and mercy that he has shown me in my life. Tupac Shakur had a poem in his poetry book "The Rose that grew though Concrete" entitled "God". His poem talked about how God was the only one there for him in his time of need. I remember him saying something about when he was alone and had nothing, and asked for a friend to help him bear the pain, no one came to him except God, and when he needed a breathe of air to rise, no one was there to give it to him except God, and when he saw so much pain and needed answers, no one answered him except God, so when people ask him who does he love unconditionally, they shouldn't expect no other name than God. Out of every thing that I've ever heard or read that Tupac has written, that poem touches my heart the most because I can remember all of the time I felt so alone and it seemed as if God was the only one that I could call on for comfort.

I think about all of the times that I felt as if I was going insane, and God gave me a peace of mind. I think about all of the times that I was to hurt to even cry, and God blessed me with the ability to write poetry as an outlet for me to release the pain that I held within. I can certainly sat that throughout all of my trials and tribulations, God has never once forsaken me, even in my times of trouble. As I sat in jail my heart would just ache with pain, and my thoughts would run wild to the point that I couldn't even sleep at night. But when I prayed and called on God from my jail cell, he answered my prayers and comforted me when no one else could. God even blessed me with the peace of mind to begin writing to pass the time away, and it was then I made up in my mind in heart that everything that I write about will be to glorify the goodness of God. Because it was then that I learned that God would never turn his back on me, even in my times of trouble.

Behold what manner of love the Father has bestowed on us,
That we should be called children of God

Therefore the world does not know us,
Because it did not know Him

Beloved, now we are children of God;
And it has not yet been revealed what we shall be,

But we know that when He is revealed, we shall be like Him,
For we shall see Him as He is

And everyone that has this hope in Him
Purifies himself

Just as He is pure

I really don't know what it is that God has planned for me in life, but I do believe that it's going to be something of greatness. I remember telling a pastor of a local church around my way that I wanted to be like him when I grew up, and he replied to me that if I'm trying to be like him then I should be okay, because he's trying to be like Jesus. After the conversation, that thought pondered in my mind and it was then I realized how important it is to be an upright role model. I began to think about all of the kids that I may have influenced in one way or another, and I just prayed that the man they may have seen me as that day was a upright man and without question a man who could be called a man of God. But since this book is being brought to you after my life has been changed, I really don't know whom the man was they may have seen at the present time.

Before I was taken away from the world, I never really realized just how many people my words have touched, just as I never really realized just how many people looked up to me as a positive male role model in the community. When I was arrested, the only thing that went through my mind was the faces of all of the kids that I may have let down. I could hear young voices in my mind saying, if Sean couldn't hold on, then how will I, especially when it was him that I have always looked towards for strength and motivation. I thought about all of the parents that I must have let down, especially the ones that may have use me to be an example to their child. So if I haven't had the opportunity to personally apologize to you, please excuse me while I take the time to say that I'm sorry. I pray that those of you who have put me on a pedestal can forgive me for my downfall. I pray that you understand that I don't expect for you to put me back on the pedestal, but I do pray that you love me enough to help me get back up off of the ground so that I may live as a child of God.

Proverbs 2:1-6

My son,
If thou wilt receive my words,
And hide my commandments with thee;

So that thou incline thine ear unto wisdom,
And apply thine heart to understanding;

Yea, if thou cries after knowledge,
And lifts up thy voice for understanding;

If thou seeks her as silver,
And searches for her as for hidden treasures;

Then shalt thou understand the fear of the Lord
And find the knowledge of God

For the Lord gives wisdom:
Out of his mouth cometh knowledge and understanding

When I began reading the bible, it was almost as if I was trying to read an foreign English language. It was like I understood most of the words, but I still couldn't understand exactly what the bible was saying. I keep on reading because I figured that sooner or later my comprehension skills would kick in and then maybe I'll have more insight on what each scripture is meant to teach me. I waited and waited on my comprehension skills to kick in, but it seems as if they never did, so like most people with short attention spans, I put the bible down. A couple of days later, I found myself writing a poem and I need to look up some facts in the bible so I began reading but I still couldn't find any true understanding in the scripture, so I just stated the facts from the bible and left it alone. At one point I felt that maybe it wasn't meant for me to understand, but I later on learned that it takes the spiritual eye to read the bible because it's a lot of things in the bible that the physical eye will never even see. Basically you gotta be able to read in-between the lines.

I remember my pastor saying in one of his sermons that we must pray for knowledge, wisdom, and understanding so that we may be able to see things through the spiritual eye and not with the physical eye. When I began to grow closer to God, I prayed for understanding and it seems as if every time I would read the bible I would begin to see things in a different manner and I began to gain more understanding of the scriptures. It was like my eyes had been opened and I was allowed to see so much more. I guess it's like I said before, I was now able to somewhat read in-between the lines. Not only did I begin to see things in the bible in a different light, I also began to see life in a different light. I began to realize that my life is supposed to have trials and tribulations, because trials and tribulations is what mold us as people. I learned that it is everything that I've been through and everything that I will go through in life will make me the man that God wants me to be.

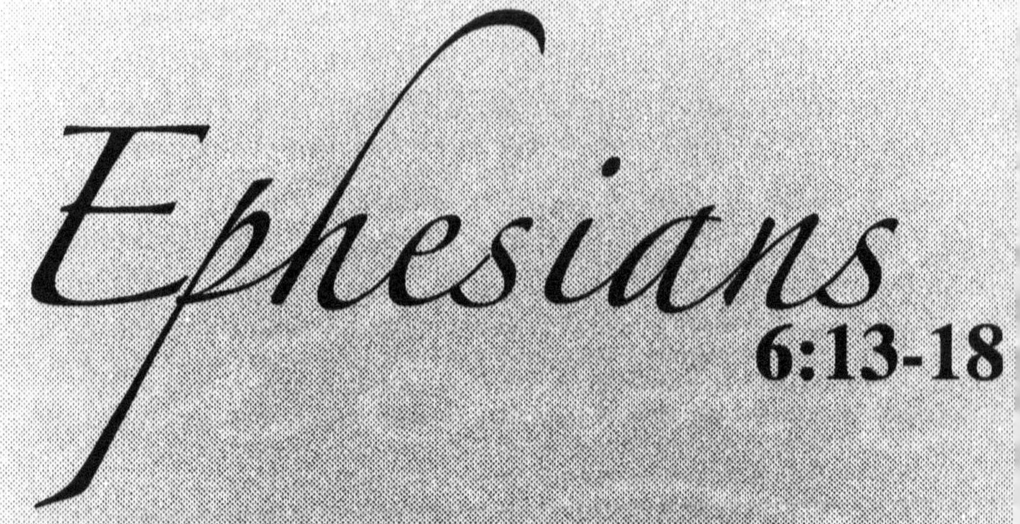

Wherefore take unto you the whole armor of God,
That you may be able to withstand in the evil day,
And having done all to stand

Stand therefore, having your loins girt about with truth,
And having on the breastplate of righteousness;

And your feet shod with the preparation of the gospel of peace;

Above all, taking the shield of faith,
Wherewith you shall be able to quench
All the fiery darts of the wicked

And take the helmet of salvation,
And the sword of the Spirit,
Which is the word of God:

Praying always with all prayer and supplication in the Spirit,
And watching with all perseverance
And supplication for all saints

All my life I have known that I have been in a battle, but it wasn't the battle that I have always thought it was. When I thought it was a battle of me against the world, I was wrong, because I later on learned in life that I was in a battle against the devil. I learned that I was in a battle between good and evil or what some may consider as a war between spirit and flesh. And just as any solider that's in battle, I would also need gear or what the bible calls the armor of God. Dating way back to the gladiator days, every fighter covered themselves with the proper armor they needed to protect themselves from their opponents weapons. And even though I may not be in a physical fight with the devil, I still need to cover my body for protection, maybe that's why I have always heard people pray for God to cover them with his blood.

The bible teaches us that the devil has come to steal, kill, and destroy, but I think that the bible forgot to add by any means necessary. Since the devil is constantly at work to destroy us, we must stay prayed up and we must always try to be protected from his weapons. Ephesians chapter six verses thirteen through eighteen shows us how we can stay protected from the devils weapon by putting on the whole armor of God. Some may take this scripture lightly but I am a living witness of what can happen to a person if they don't protect themselves from the devil. It's just like a policeman running into a shoot-out with out a bullet proof vest or like a fireman running into a burning building without his or her fire suit on, that out come might not be that pretty if you know what I'm saying. Think about if you were a running back going against the number one defense in the nation without your helmet or pads, that's the same way that you can look at it going against the devil without the armor of God. Just as a running back you will need your helmet, your breastplate or shoulder pads, and you will also need some good shoes for your feet, but most of all you will need heart, or shall I say that you will need God in your heart to be able to withstand in the evil day.

Matthew 6:5-8

When you pray, you shall not be like the hypocrites
For they love to pray in the churches and on the street corners
That they may be seen by men
Assuredly, I say to you, they have their reward

But when you pray, go into your room,
And when you have shut your door,
Pray to your Father who sees in secretly
Will reward you openly

And when you pray, do not use vain repetitions
As the heathens do, for they think
That they will be heard for their many words

Therefore do not be like them
For your Father knows the things you have need of
Before you even ask Him

The bible teaches us that when prayers go up, blessings will come back down. But the bible also teaches us that it's certain ways you must pray if you want God to hear and answer your prayers. The scripture says that we should not pray vain repetitious prayers, and we should not pray just to be seen by the people of the church or the world. The bible teaches us that we should pray secretly behind closed doors, because God already knows your hearts needs before you even ask them of him. God said that whosoever pray to him sincere in secret, shall be rewarded by him openly.

Have you ever known one of them so called saints that call on God out loud during the church service, and then when the opportunity presents itself they jump up and run around the church shouting claiming to be full of the Holey Ghost, but as soon as they leave the church grounds they light up a cigarette and it seems as if every other word that comes out of their mouth is a curse word. Now I know that I can't be the only one who has ever seen this happen, so if you have seen it happen also, those are the people that just do it for show, and not for the glory of God.

This scripture also teaches us that we should not use vain repetitious prayers, meaning that we shouldn't be praying for just the things of the world such as money, cars, or whatever other material thing that you can think of. God also said that we shouldn't pray in repetitions, meaning that we shouldn't keep saying the same thing over and over again in the same prayer, I guess some people believe that the longer the prayer is, the more God will bless you, but the bible says otherwise. I believe that one should just pray completely from the heart, as a matter of fact, I don't even consider myself to be praying, because I just talk to God just as if I was talking to my best friend, because in all actuality, that's exactly what I'm doing.

I waited patiently for the Lord;
And he inclined unto me,
And heard my cry

He brought me up also out of an horrible pit,
Out of the miry clay, and set my feet upon a rock,
And established my goings

And he hath put a new song in my mouth,
Even praise unto our God:
Many shall see it, and fear, and shall trust in the Lord

Blessed is the man that makes the Lord his trust,
And respects not the proud, nor such as turn aside to lies

I remember when I use to constantly laugh just to keep from constantly crying. And I remember always hearing people say that joy would cometh in the morning light, so I patiently waited, but it seemed as if that morning would never come for me. I remember the times that I would cry out to God because I didn't know what else to do, but it seemed as if he would never answer me. And I remember the times I found myself lost in the dark and it seemed as if I would never find my way out, so I begged God to please come and show me the way, but it was like he never came. I remember times I would cry out to God, asking him why has he forsaken me at the times I needed him most, but I got no response from him. But guess what, I later on learned in life that God was right there with me the whole time, its like the poem Footprints sated, when I looked down and saw only one set of footprints, it wasn't that God had forsaken me and left me to walk alone, but it was when God was carrying me through the things that he knew was to much for me to bear, so therefore the footprints that I saw in the sand wasn't my own, but they were the footprints of God.

I learned that every hurdle that I was forced to jump in life; it was God who gave me the strength to get over them. Every maze that I had to walk through in the dark; it was God who gave me light and opened my eyes so I could see my way safely through. Every downfall in my life was perfectly designed to teach me how to get back up again, and every tear that I may have shed through the years has cleansed my eyes so I may see that much better. The bible teaches us that all things in our life works for the greater good, even though we may not be able to understand it at that present time. I know it gets hard sometimes, but I promise you that if you patiently wait on God, he will deliver you from all of your troubles, no matter what they may be.

Deuteronomy
32:6-8

Do you thus deal with the Lord,
O foolish and unwise people?

Is He not your Father who has bought you?

Has He not made you and established you?

Remember the days of old,
Consider the years of many generations

Ask your Father,
And he will show you

Ask your Elders,
And they will tell you

How may times have you heard someone older say; I wish I would have known then, what it is that I know now. I wish I would have listened and understood then, because if I had, then I know that I wouldn't be going through the things that I am now. A poet named Ron Henderson said that B.I.B.L.E stands for Basic Instructions Before Leaving Earth, and if you really think about it, that's exactly what it is. The bible is like a manual written by your spiritual father, who is God, and supposed to be taught to you by your physical father so that you may understand life. It's just like if you bought a bookshelf that needs to be put together, the company will send a manual along with the bookshelf so that you may have instructions and examples to go by to make putting together the bookshelf that much easier.

The bible teaches us that whenever we don't have a complete understanding of something, we should ask our Father and he will show us, and if we should have any further questions, we should ask our elders, and they will tell us. The same exact rules apply with the bible as it does with the bookshelf. If you are reading the bible or shall I say your life manual, and you don't seem to understand exactly what it is saying, then pray and ask God for knowledge and understanding, and he will open your eyes so that you may better understand. And if you are beginning to understand but there are some questions that you have, then you should ask your elders, and they will tell you the answers to your questions. I believe that if we all were willing to help and share information with one another, we would be a much stronger community, especially the black community. And if would continued this tradition of sharing with one another, then I'm sure it will trickle down to generation to generation, which will one day establish a better society just as it was meant to be.

I am forgotten as a dead man out of mind:

I am like a broken vessel

For I have heard the slander of many:
And fear was on every side:

While they took counsel together against me,
They devised to take away my life

But I trusted in thee,
O Lord: I said,
Thou art my God

My times are in thy hand:
Deliver me from the hand of mine enemies,
And from them that persecute me

Before April twenty-fourth, two thousand and three, you would have thought that I was Gods gift to the world. It was then that I was a writer, poet, author, and even actor. I co-hosted a local TV show with my partners Azhea, and Nico on the set of Soul Ave. I owned and operated my very own publishing company that I started from scratch, and I was even doing book tours up and down the East coast, and I even stepped into the Midwest a time or two. I have sold books as far as Africa and the United Kingdom and I was even planning to tour Europe in the next year or so. It seemed as if all the ladies loved me, and I had more friends than I could count. People around the world praised me because of my writing ability, and supported me like you wouldn't believe. But on April twenty-fifth, it would all change because I was no longer the writer that every one seemed to love, I was then the criminal that no one wanted anything to do with.

People can say what they want to say about me, but they can never say that I don't speak the truth and that I don't speak from the heart. So let me tell you how it is, because when it's good it's good, and everybody's there with you to enjoy your success, but when hard times come, it seems as if everybody leaves you to go find some one else who is successful. I stood in the court room with nothing but a judge in front of me, a hand full of family members behind me, and three friends beside me as the four of us stood there, listening to the judge say that we a facing twenty-five years to life for armed robbery.
I spent a little over a month in jail, and then I was finally released to be on twenty-four hour house arrest while I waited for trial. While I was home, it seemed as if the phone would never ring, and those that swear they loved me seemed to turn their backs on me. But it seemed when everyone was against me, God came to my aid and delivered me. That's why I put all of my trust in God, because he has never failed me nor forsaken me.

For great is thy mercy toward me:
And thou hast delivered my soul from the lowest hell

O God, the proud are risen against me,
And the assemblies of violent men have sought after my soul;
And have not set thee before them

But thou, O Lord, art a God full of compassion,
And gracious, long-suffering, and plenteous in mercy and truth

O turn unto me, and have mercy upon me;
Give thy strength unto thy servant,
And save the son of thine handmaid

Show me a token for good;
That they which hate me may see it, and be ashamed:
Because thou, Lord, hast helped me, and comforted me

Have you ever really thought about just how compassionate and merciful God actually is? Think about all of the times that you have sinned in your life, and then think about all of the times that you have asked for forgiveness and God forgave you. The bible teaches us that no matter what we've done wrong, if we should sincerely ask God for forgiveness, he will cast our sins out into the sea of forgiveness, and the sins will be remembered no more. Now how merciful is that? I truly thank God for his grace and mercy, and all of the times that he has forgiven me for the many sins that I may have committed. I thank God for delivering me when I was in the lowest hell on earth, now I don't know about to you, but to me jail is the lowest hell that I can think of on this earth, but God continued to bless me even in my times of trouble he stayed right by my side to comfort me.

God even showed me a token for good, and just as the scripture read; those that hated me saw it and was ashamed, because when it seemed that I was down and out, God helped me, comforted me, and raised me to heights higher than I've ever known before. It seemed that when I told people that I was coming out with a new book, they seemed confused, I guess they wondered how could I so quickly write and release a book when I have been incarcerated and on house arrest for most of all of two thousand and three. If it's one thing that I've learned in the past year, it is that if you work for the good of God, then God will surely work for the good of you. I remember a conversation that I had with Omar Tyree when I was on house arrest, and I remember him telling me that I should use this time I had for the good. Basically he was telling me that I had two choices with my situation, I could either pout about being on house arrest and benefit nothing, or I could use the time I had constructively, by writing and thinking of new creative ideas that would benefit me later on when I came out of my situation. So thank God and him if you enjoy this book.

Having the understanding darkened and being alienated
From the life of God through the ignorance that is in them,
Because of the blindness of their heart:

Who being past feeling have given themselves over unto
lasciviousness, to work all uncleanness with greediness

But you have not learned Christ;

If so be that you have heard him,
And have been taught by him,
As the truth is in Jesus:

That you put off concerning
The former conversation the old man,
Which is corrupt according to the deceitful lusts;
And be renewed in the spirit of your mind;
And that you put on the new man,
Which after God is created in righteousness and true holiness

I have always heard that in order for there to be life, there also must be death, because life and death are both within the three hundred and sixty degrees cycle of life. The same rules apply with good and evil and spirit and flesh. In order for you to be spiritually born again, you must first allow your old fleshly ways to die. In the sight of God, there is no in between, because either you are going to live in the light with God, or you are going to continue living in the dark with the devil. God said that those people who say they know him and lives in the dark is a liar, because he is the light and if you live in the dark, you can't know the light.

Everyday I struggle trying to find my way completely out of the dark. But I thank God for bringing me this far, but I know that I have so much farther to go. I know that in order for me to be spiritually born again, I must allow the old me to die. I know that I have a lot of bad habits that I must do away with. I also must be able to let go of all of the anger that I once held in my heart, and allow God to fill my heart with love. I must be willing to let down the barriers that I have placed around me, and learn to trust and not believe that everyone is out to bring me down. I also must be willing to let go of all of the things I lust after, such as the women and the finer things in life, and learn to want for nothing of the earth. I must be willing to open my arms to strangers and even my enemies, because God said that we should have compassion in our hearts and we should love even our enemies.

My fellow poet Tim Jackson once asked; how many of my people are willing to die for God, and in my heart I said I would. But another poet by the name of Woman Storm made a statement that it may be easier for us to say that we will die for God, than it is for us to say that we will live for God. Just think to yourself, are you really willing to live for God.

Be merciful unto me, O God:
For man would swallow me up; he fighting daily oppresses me

Mine enemies would daily swallow me up:
For they be many that fight against me, O thou most High

What time I am afraid, I will trust in thee

In God I will praise his word, in God I have put my trust'
I will not fear what flesh can do unto me

Every day they wrest my words:
All their thoughts are against me for evil

They gather themselves together,
They hide themselves, they mark my steps,
When they wait for my soul

Shall they escape by iniquity?
In thine anger cast down the people O God

Sometimes I just sit back and think about where I could or would be if it wasn't for Gods grace ad mercy. If you have been reading this book you may have realized that I haven't always walked on the good foot, or even down the right path. I think about the times that I have been in the wrong place at the wrong time and I have heard bullets whistling in my hear, but I left the scene without a scratch on my body, now I know that it wasn't anything more to it than Gods grace and mercy. I think about all of the car accidents that I've been in, and when I think about the condition of the car that I walked away from, I know that it was Gods grace and mercy because if you looked at the condition of the car then you may have also thought to yourself, how in the world did he make it out of that. Well first of all, I myself didn't make it out; it was truly Gods grace and mercy that brought me out of all the situations that I have had no control over.

Webster defines grace as an unmerited help given to people by God (as in overcoming temptation). Grace is also defined as freedom from sin through dive grace, and as a virtue coming from God. Webster defines mercy as a blessing resulting from divine favor or compassion, such as compassion shown to victims of misfortune. Mercy can also be compassion shown to an offender, such as imprisonment to someone that has committed first-degree murder instead of giving the death penalty. Just as God feels sympathetic towards us and our sins, the judge may also feel sympathetic towards the offender depending on the circumstances of the crime that has been committed or for better words, the reason that the crime was committed. Aren't you glad that God loves us enough to forgive us for our sins, knowing that we could a lot worst off in life than we are. Just think about where you could be or would be if it wasn't for Gods grace and mercy.

Mark 11:22-26

And Jesus answering said unto them,
Have faith in God

For verily I say unto you,
That whosoever shall say unto this mountain,
Are thou removed,
And be cast into the sea; and shall not doubt in his hear,
But shall believe that those things
Which he said shall come to pass;
He shall have whatsoever he said

Therefore I say unto you, what things so ever you desire,
When you pray, believe that you will receive them,
And you shall have them

And when you stand praying, forgive,
If you have ought against any:
That your Father also which is in heaven
May forgive you your trespasses

But if you do not forgive,
Neither will your Father, which is in heaven
Forgive your trespasses

I bet that if I asked you do you believe in God, you would probably say yes, but if I asked you do you believe that you can walk on water, you would probably look at me as if I am crazy. So I guess my question to you is, just how much do you really believe in God, because if you truly believe in God, then there is no reason that you shouldn't believe that you can walk on water because the bible teaches us that through God all things are possible. I'm not saying the next time you go to the ocean step out of the boat or anything like that, but I am saying that I don't think that a lot of us believe in God the way that we think that we believe in him. I remember back when me and my partners use to jump anything that we could find, we would jump fences, ditches, and we would even jump the gas tank in my grandfathers back yard. As a kid I had no fear or shall I say that I had all the faith in the world that I could jump whatever was put in front of me, but as I got a little older I didn't have the same confidence that I did as a kid. Remember when you would prepare to jump a fence or something and you would take off running from a good distance to gain speed to help you over your obstacle, but as soon as you get to the fence you pull back because of the fear that quickly ran across your mind, I believe that the same principles applies with God.

Faith is defined as being complete trust or believing and trusting inn God. I truly believe I my heart that faith conquers all. Think about it, faith is what allowed David to defeat Goliath, faith allowed Michael Jordan to become on of the greatest basketball players in the world, faith also allowed Oprah Winfrey to be able to own herself and become one of the wealthiest people in the world, and faith is also what allowed Jay-Z to overcome the obstacles that was placed in front of him to become one of the greatest lyricist and businessmen in the hip-hop industry. Though all of these people excelled in different areas, it was their faith that allowed them to keep on pushing on when they may have wanted to give up.

Psalms
88:1-7

O Lord God of my salvation,
I have cried day and night before thee:

Let my prayer come before thee:
Incline thine ear unto my cry;

For my soul is full of troubles:
And my life draws nigh unto the grave

I am counted with them that do down into the pit:
I am as a man that hath no strength:

Free among the dead, like the slain that lie in the grave,
Whom thou remember no more:
And they are cut off from thy hand

Thou hast laid me in the lowest pit, in darkness, in the deeps

Thy wrath lies hard upon me,
And thou hast afflicted me with all thy waves

Selah

Some people have criticized me on my writing style saying that I say inappropriate things while I'm talking to God, and I can understand why they may feel that way. But please understand why I feel the way I feel and why I write the way that I do. I believe that we all are sinners in one way or another regardless if people want to admit it or not, as a matter of fact even the bible says that we are all sinners, so the question isn't whether or not you are a sinner, the question is do have a need to be righteous. The bible teaches me that God already knows what's in my heart and what my needs are before I even bend down on my knees and talk to him. The bible also teaches me that I should confess to God completely and whole-heartedly if I wish for him to hear my cry. So that's what I do, I release all of the pain and the anger that's being held in my heart and I place all of the burdens that I have in my life in Gods hand, and I leave it all at the alter because God said that's what I should do, so that's what I do.

I remember the times in my life that I just wanted to end it all, and I remember falling on my knees praying that God understood why I felt the way that I did. The strange thing about it was whenever I got up off of my knees, the need to end it all was gone, and as a matter of fact I felt as if the weight of the world had been lifted off of my shoulders. Maybe I felt that way because I had left all of my frustrations with God, and maybe he felt that it was more on me than I could bear so therefore it took off of me what I couldn't handle myself. It seemed as if after I prayed I could see a life worth living, as before all I could see was death. I have often thought to myself how low must a person feel to actually go through with the process of committing suicide, because I have been to the point of wanting to die and I know how low I felt, but to actually commit suicide, is a feeling that even I can't imagine. So the next time you see somebody that seems to feel down and out, please say some encouraging words to them, because you could actually save their life and not even know it.

I John 1:1-10

This is the message that we have heard of him,
And declared to you,

God is the light,
And in him is no darkness at all

If we say we fellowship with him, and walk in darkness,
We are liars, and have not told the truth:
But if we walk in the light, for that he is in the light

We have fellowshipped with one another
And the blood of his son Jesus Christ cleans us from all sins

If we say that we have no sins, we deceive ourselves,
And the truth will not be in us
But if we confess our sins,
He is faithful and quick to forgive us,
And cleanse us from all that is unrighteous

If we say that we have not sinned,
We make him a liar, and his word is not in us

When I first read this scripture the first thing that came to my mind was how can one win without losing when it comes to God. I was so confused because I couldn't understand exactly what God was saying. It's like if you are a sinner then you can't know God, and if you are a sinner and say that you know God then you are a liar, but it also says that if you say that you are not a sinner then you are still a liar, because God says that we all are sinners, so how can we win without losing. It seems to me that what God is really saying in this scripture is to be real with yourself. If you know that you are a sinner don't act like you're a saint, because you may be able to lie to the rest world, but you can't lie to yourself and especially not God.

The scripture says that if we say that we have no sins, then we deceive ourselves, and the truth will not be in us. But if we confess our sins, God will be faithful and quick to forgive us of our sins and cleanse us from all that is unrighteous, so the best thing for you to do is to be open and honest with God. The next time you pray try being real with yourself and God, and see don't you see some changes take place in your life. And when you pray, talk to God just as if you were talking to that best friend that you know you can confide in. If you know that you have made some mistakes in your life, then just say God I messed up and I'm sorry, and I pray that you forgive me, and the rest will be history because God will cast your sin out into the sea of forgiveness to be remembered no more. Don't forget that we serve a compassionate and merciful God that is willing to forgive you. No matter what you may have done in life, remember that there is no sin that is bigger or smaller than another sin in the eyes of God. I think that some people feel that they are okay just because they haven't committed crimes such as murder or armed robbery, but the bible says that those crimes are in the same boat with what some may consider as a simple white lie. Basically a sin is a sin in Gods sight, no matter how you may try to look at it.

Thou tallest my wanderings:
Put thou my tears into thy bottle:
Are they not in thy book?

When I cry into thee,
Then shall mine enemies turn back:
This I know; for God is for me

In God will I praise his word:
In the Lord will I praise his word

In God have I put my trust:
I will not be afraid what man can do unto me

Thy vows are upon me, O God,
I will render praises unto thee

For thou hast delivered my soul from death:
Wilt not thou deliver my feet from falling,
That I may walk before God in the light of the living

The bible teaches us that if God is for us, which he is, then there is no man that can be against us. I remember standing in the courtroom in front of the chief judge at my pretrial plea hearing, and all I could hear in my mind was my lawyer saying the day before that I was going to be held in custody, because this judge had never released someone that was facing the charges that I was facing back on house arrest. I also remember my cousin telling me that at his plea hearing, the same judge sent word to me that I should be ready to stay in jail when I come to court because he didn't feel that I should be out on pretrial house arrest anyway. My cousin was in the same boat that I was in, because he was also released to be put on pretrial house arrest, but when he went back to court for his plea hearing, the judge locked him back up so therefore I was expecting the same thing to happen to me.

Psalms fifty-six taught me that If I cried out to God, then my enemies would turn back because they would know that God was for me. So therefore I put all of my trust in God and walked in the courtroom without a fear in my heart. It seemed as if everything that my cousin and my lawyer told me was irrelevant to me at that point in time. I stood before the judge with God on one side of me and my lawyer on the other, and all I could think about was the promise that I made to God. I had promised God about a week before my court date that if he allowed me to come back home to complete this book, then I would make sure that his word got out through every word that I would ever write or speak from that point on. I promised God that everything I did in the way of writing would be used to the uplifting of his kingdom, but I would be doing it in a way that I felt would reach the masses and not just one group of people. It was only because of Gods grace and mercy that I have presented this book to you, because it was God who allowed me to come back home and finish it.

But unto thee have I cried, O Lord;
And in the morning shall my prayer prevent thee

Lord, why castest thou off my soul?
Why hidest thou thy face from me?

I am afflicted and ready to die from my youth up:
While I suffer thy terrors I am distracted

Thy fierce wrath goes over me;
Thy terrors have cut me off

They came round about me daily like water;
They compassed me about together

Lover and friend hast thou put far from me,
And mine acquaintance into darkness

Psalms eighty-eight is described as being a prayer of despondency, which despondency has been defined by Webster as a feeling of hopelessness or when you feel that you are at your lowest in spirits. I think that we all have felt despondent at times, and our faith seems to have stood on unstable grounds. I remember when I felt despondent and it seemed as everyone had left me to fight against the world on my own. I would call on God but it seemed as if he would never answer me. I would look towards my elders for help and answers but it seemed as if no one had time to spare with me. I would even look towards my female friends for a shoulder to cry on, but it seemed that they were no longer around. I felt that if the whole world had turned it's back on me, so therefore I just yelled out fuck the world.

I began to rebel and lose faith in God maybe because I felt that he had lost faith in me. I also felt that maybe that was why everyone else had turned their back on me, because they had lost faith in me too. And it seems as if when everyone loses faith in you, you also begin to lose faith in yourself. I remember times in my life that I felt so hopeless that all I wanted to do was to go to sleep and never wake up again. You couldn't even imagine how many nights I sat alone in my room praying that God would take me peacefully in my sleep because I didn't want to face the world another day, it seemed as if I wanted everyday to be my last day.

Now that I have pasted that point in my life, I truly thank God that he never answered my prayers to die. The bible says that God will never give you more than you can bear, but he will allow you to reach your limit. I believe that, that's the way that God test our faith in him, and if we have enough faith in him to persevere and not curse his name, then God will bring us out of the situation that we are in and bless us for being faithful.

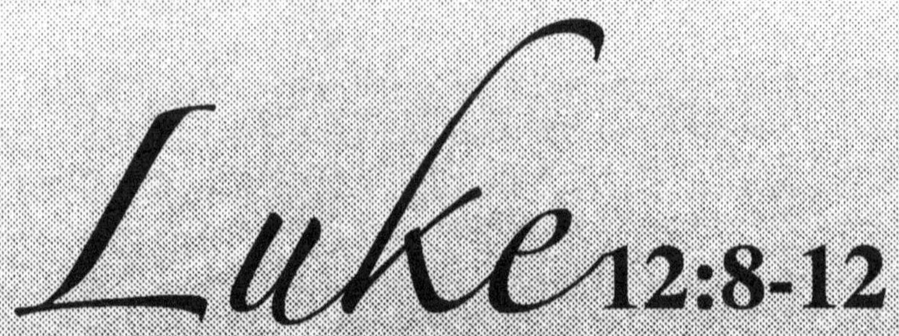# Luke 12:8-12

I say unto you,
Whosoever shall confess me before men,
The Son of God shall confess him before the angels of God:

But he that denies me before men,
Shall be denied before the angels of God

And whosoever shall speak a word against the Son of man,
Shall be forgiven:
But he who blasphemes against the Holy Ghost,
Shall not be forgiven

And when they bring you in front of the congregation,
Unto the magistrates, and the powers that be,
Have no thought on how or what things you shall answer,
Or even what you will say:

For the Holy Ghost shall teach you
What you should say with in the same hour

As long as I have air in my lungs and blood in my heart, I will confess the goodness of God through my poetry whether the media or the masses likes it or not. I have often seen entertainers such as hip-hop artist shunned by the public when they would rap about their spiritual beliefs. So therefore a lot of them talk about killing, sex, drugs, and whatever other stories they may have heard or seen on the news just so they can create record sales. My home girl Tina wrote a poem titled Idol concerning this very matter. Her poem talks about how the youth of the world idolize many hip-hop artist just because they have been shot up a couple of times, or because they have spent a couple of years in prison. Trust me, if that artist has killed as many people as he say he has, then I promise you that he would not be walking the streets today, especially when you have the FBI in the world.

Tina goes on to say that maybe if God was shot up rather than being hung up, then maybe he could also get some love from the streets. Maybe if God said he's been locked up for the last five thousand years, then maybe he could be a real nigga just like some of these fake ass rappers. But I guess they do what they gotta do to eat, because we all know that sex sales better than God does. I'm not knocking a person for doing what they gotta do, but I am saying that when you are put in a position to influence the world by media, you should think about the representation that you are showing to all of the people that may look towards you as a leader and an idol. It's funny to me to hear an artist talk about everything else in their album except God, but as soon as they win an award the first person they wanna thank is God. Maybe they truly do have God within their hearts but they're afraid to confess him before men because they're afraid that their tough guy image will be shattered which will cause record sales to go down. But Jesus said that if we don't confess him before men, then he won't confess us before the angels of God.

Defend me from mine enemies, O my God,
Defend me from them that rise up against me

Deliver me from the workers of iniquity,
And save me from bloody me

For look, they lie in wait for my soul:
The mighty are gathered against me:
Not for my transgression,
Nor for my sin, O Lord

They run and prepare themselves without my fault:
Awake to help me, and behold

Thou therefore, O Lord God of hosts,
The God of Israel, awake to visit all the heathen:
Be not merciful to any wicked transgressors

Selah

I have always heard elders say that when things happen and innocent people die, that just means that the devil is steadily working or what I like to call working overtime. It seems that the closer a person gets to God, the more enemies the devil send their way to steal from them, kill them, or destroy them in one way or another. Just as God places his people in our lives to help us make it through our spiritual journey, the devil places his people in our lives also to make sure that we are knock off course while we are trying to travel the roads to Zion. Even though God says that we should love our enemies, he also knows that we should also be aware of whom our enemies are, because your enemy could be the very person that you would give the shirt off of your back because it seems as if they would do the same for you.

The devil has taught his people how to be patient and wait on the right time when it seems that you are very despondent, and when you are at your lowest point in life, they are trained to attack you in the most tactful way. Whether we want to realize it or not, your enemy could be one of your family members such as your parents or siblings, or it could be that person that you have known your whole life and considers them as a best friend. Your enemy could also be that person that you just meet one day and it seems that you and them have a lot in common so therefore you let down your guards and invite them into your circle. Or your enemy could be that person you met of the opposite sex who has seemed to find you at the right moment in your life, normally that moment is when you feel afraid and alone. The devil is to smart to us someone that is your personal enemy because he knows that you are expecting for them to try to hurt you, so that's why he uses someone that you would never expect, someone that is very close to you. That's why they say that you should keep your friends close, but your enemies even closer. But don't worry because God said that he will protect us from all of our enemies, even the devils people.

Thou hast put away mine acquaintance far from me;
Thou hast made me an abomination unto them:
I am shut up, and I cannot come forth.

Mine eye mourns by reason of affliction:
Lord, I have called daily upon thee,
I have stretched out my hands unto thee

Wilt thou show wonders to the dead?
Shall the dead arise and praise thee?

Shall thy loving kindness be declared in the grave?
Or thy faithfulness in destruction?

Shall thy wonders be known in the dark?
And thy righteousness in the land of forgetfulness

When I stood in the midst of my trials and tribulations it seems as if those that personally knew me, backed away from me as if they were disgusted with the mistakes that I had made in my life. Maybe they felt that being associated with a criminal such as myself would taint their image. Even though a lot of people turned their back on me, I still didn't feel forsaken because I knew that God would continue to stand by my side. I felt so distant from some people that I really didn't know what to say to some of the same people that I had known for years, maybe because I felt that no matter what I said, the image that they had in their mind of me would stay the same.

The Wilson Daily Times had painted a portrait that was so ugly of me that I myself couldn't even stand to read it. The article on my case totally shattered my name and my reputation. I began to think that I would never be able to bounce back from this kind of situation, especially being that so many people knew me personally and as an author and as an entertainer. All I could think about was the faces of the kids that would see this newspaper article, and how I must have let them down as a leader and as a role model. I thought about all of the people that have put me on a pedestal at one time or another in my career saying that the world needs more positive young black males like myself, and there I was in the newspaper facing charges of armed robbery. At first I felt ashamed to go back into the world and face the people that thought so much of me as a person and an author. When I was released on house arrest, I was allowed to go to church, and at first I didn't really want to go because I was afraid that so many people would be pointing fingers at me and talking about me because of the mistakes that I had made in my life. But some way some how, God allowed me to face the world with my head held high because I knew that only God could judge me for my sins, because he's the only one that will forgive me.

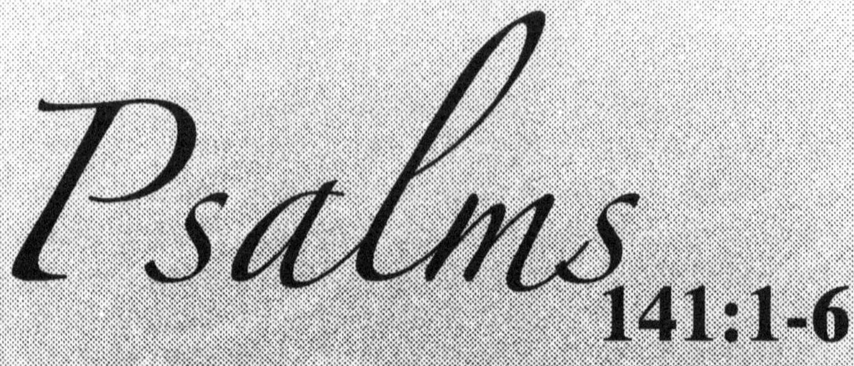

Psalms 141:1-6

Lord, I cry unto thee: make haste unto me;
Give ear unto my voice, when I cry unto thee

Let my prayer be set forth before thee as incense;
And the lifting up of my hands as the evening sacrifice

Set a watch, O Lord, before my mouth;
Keep the door of my lips

Incline not my heart to any evil thing,
To practice wicked works with men that work iniquity:
And let me not eat of their dainties

Let the righteous smite me; it shall be kindness:
And let him reprove me; it shall be excellent oil,
Which shall not break my head:
For yet my prayer also shall be in their calamities

When their judges are overthrown in stony places,
They shall hear my words; for they are sweet

This book has been a testimony of my life, and how gracious and merciful God has been to me through the years. I have shared my life with you through my poetry books, my audio books, and through every poem or story that I have ever written in the hope that it may inspire someone that may be going through their own personal trials and tribulations. I pray that you understand that every time I step foot on a stage to perform, my mission is to bring a lost soul closer to God, because I feel in my heart that's what God has chosen me to do in life. I share my life with you because I know that I am an example of just how good God is, and no matter what you may be going through in life, God will see that you make it through. Trust me because I know first hand.

I've done all I known to do to prevail in life, but now I know that without God in my life, I can never prevail. Some may look at me and think that life is just full of joy because I always seem to keep a smile on my face, but they just don't know how much pain and anger that my heart once held. I laughed just to keep from crying, but I knew that one day it would all be released in one-way or another. But I learned to leave it all in Gods hands.

When I was younger I released my pain and anger in the way of violence, but as I grew older I began to release my pain and anger in the way of words. I remember when Ms.. Sutton use to constantly tell me how gifted of a writer I was, and how I could use my gift to benefit not only myself, but I could also benefit others by touching hearts and opening minds with my words. Maybe that's why I wouldn't only cry for myself but I would also begin to cry for others. It seemed the more I would write, the more burdens I would put on my shoulders, because not did I carry around my own problems, but now I began to carry around the problems of every little boy and girl that seems to be traveling the same unbeaten path as I once did.

POETIC PRAYERS

OF A FALLEN ANGEL

<u>Born to Write</u>

Why can't you understand that I was born to do this
Before I was even born

And when I'm dead and gone my people
My words will continue to live on

Because I'm so far ahead of my time
I have already written books to be released here
While I'm chilling in heaven in my after life

I have already made future preparations to gain currency
To take care of my future kids and wife
After I leave this life

And know that I do thank you for your kind words and support
But please don't praise me for the words
That had already been written

Honestly, I'm just copying what God
Had already etched in the stone tablets of my diary
So therefore, every word that I write and say has been bitten

And the fact that God wrote it on stone tablets
Means that it had already been copy written

I've already told yall that I'm just a vessel
For the words that God has given to me

And I'm sorry if I'm to deep for you to understand
But this is something that you gotta read between the lines

And if you still can't understand
That just means that yall ain't ready for me

And neither you nor the devil can stop me
From being what God has destined for me to be

You know they say the truth hurts
And maybe that's why your attention gets up and leave
As soon as I step foot on a stage

Or maybe that's why your eyes shed tears
After seeing the words that I have written on a page

Maybe that's why when you speak to me
You can't even look me in the eyes
Cause you know I can see right into your soul

And yeah I got dealt a misdealt hand at birth
But lets play on player
Cause Sean will never fold

I walk by faith
So therefore I live for the moment
And I just pray to grow old

And I no longer need to keep heaters by my side
Cause now that I have God in my life
The world no longer seems to be that cold

I mean lets cut to the chase
And lets let the truth be told

Sean Ingram Will Never Lose

<u>How am I innocent until proven guilty?</u>

How am I innocent until proven guilty
When you lock me up, before you even ask me my last name

Then you dig up information on my family and childhood
And proclaim my father to be the blame

But when I ask you what have I done wrong
You tell me that I fit the description of the man
Who pulled the trigger

But in all honesty,
The only description that I fit in your eyes
Is just that of another young poor black nigger

So how am I innocent until proven guilty?

How am I innocent until proven guilty
When you throw my mugshot on the news for the world to see

Then you place me as the prime suspect
For crimes and situations that don't even concern me

You say it was a drug deal that had gone bad
But how can that be when it were no drugs even involved

So now my lawyer is telling me
That you're connecting me with drugs and murders
That has gone for years unsolved

So how am I innocent until proven guilty?

How am I innocent until proven guilty?

When I sit behind these bars
Crying out my innocence with no voice

And it hurts me to my heart to give up on freedom
But reality is that I ain't got no other choice

So now I'm adapting to my environment
Day by day just so I can survive

Now I'm counting the years day by day
Until my 3-year-old little girl turns 25

But it seems the more that time passes behind these bars
The more God allows me to see

That just because I'm locked down physically
Doesn't mean that spiritually and mentally I can't be free

Because in Gods eyes
I am innocent until proven guilty

So therefore I will always be free
No matter what prison they try to stick me in

And no I won't beg for mercy before the judge
Because only God can forgive me for my sins

<u>All I See Is Me</u>

I'm really trying to figure out
Why so many young people wanna be like me

When I myself don't even want to be like me

 I find myself just looking in the mirror at times
To catch a glance at what they see
But all I seem to see is me

All I see is a man
Who was forced to walk on his own
Since he was eight years old

All I see is a man
Who tears blended in with the rain
And heart numbed by the cold

All I see is a man
Who hustled and scrambled
Just to be considered as broke

All I see is a man
Who laughs to keep from crying,
Cause his life has been nothing but a joke

All I see is a man
Who prays at night,
Just asking God to keep him strong

All I see is a man
Who contemplates suicide,
Cause he don't know if this is where he belong

All I see is a man
Who tears want even fall anymore

All I see is a man
Who suffers now,
Because of the mistakes that he made as a little boy

All I see is a man
Who tries to do good,
But the good is never good enough

All I see is a man
Who truly defines the meaning
Of being a diamond in the ruff

So I still can't understand
Why so many young people wanna be like me

When I myself don't even want to like me

And I'm still standing in this mirror
To catch a glance at what they see
But all I seem to see is me

And the truth is
I really don't like what I see

<u>The Stand Off</u>

And there I was,
Face to face with the barrel of his gun

But the problems that I had in my life at the time
Numbed my body, so therefor I couldn't even run

So we stood there,
Me looking at him as he was looking at me

Both thinking the same thing
Damn dawg, is this the way it gotta be?

And through the reflection of the tears
That ran slowly from my eyes

He begin to see the pains of my life
As he began to hear the voice of my grandmother cries

Saying something like
Why did my baby boy have to die?

So he tried to step back, but the problems of his life
Wouldn't even let him move

His flesh and spirit was at war
And I'm just standing there praying
Lord knows I hope that his spirit don't lose

So I began quoting scriptures
As his flesh and spirit continued to fight

And asked God to forgive us both
And prayed that he would save two young souls
tonight

Guns raised

As we stood toe to toe,
But now seeing eye to eye

Both hearts crying out for help
Cause nether one of us wants to see the other die

Cause the truth of the matter is
I don't want to kill him,
No more than he wants to kill me

And at that moment we both lowered our guns
Because we both realized,
That this ain't the way God wants it to be

Because instead of us
Spraying one another

God would rather for us to be
Praying for one another

<u>What should I say?</u>

I'm sick and tired of people asking me why don't I talk much
Ain't it obvious that I ain't got nothing to say

And when I do try to talk to you,
Your to busy or care less to understand
So that's why I just say nothing and wait until I pray

And the next time you ask me how I'm doing
Don't be surprised if I really tell you how I feel

And if you can't handle it, then I'm sorry
But as my young people say, I Gotta Keep It Real

Because reality is
Right now, I don't really know if I want to live or die

All I really know is
The hurt, hurts to bad for me to even cry

All I really know is
The niggas that grew up with me is gone,
In one way or another

And that I can see the same hunger that I had,
In the eyes of my little brother

All I really know is
That my father was never there,
And my momma was there only part time

And I thought that I found more love in the streets
Than at I did at home,
And it seemed as if nothing paid more than crime

All I really know is
That when I needed a shoulder to cry on
There was no one around

Just as when I needed a helping hand
To get back on my feet
There was no one to be found

So the next time you ask me how I'm doing
Don't be surprised if I really tell you how I feel

And if you can't handle it, then I'm sorry
But as my young people say, I Gotta Keep It Real

And reality is,
Only God has never forsaken me
No matter what I may have been going through

So that's why I rather spend my time
Talking to God than wasting time talking to you

So that's why I just say nothing
And wait until I have a quiet moment to pray

Because I know that the truth hurts
And that's how I know
That you probably don't want to hear what I got to say

<u>These Words</u>

I'm sorry if my poetry isn't cute to you
But I know nothing about whispering winds
Or pretty little butterflies

Because all I've ever known about in my life
Is that cold ass rain coming from them dark ass skies

Just as Tim Jackson said,
I ain't got time to be sitting down
Writing no pretty little rhyme skits just to amuse you

And you can say what you wanna say about me,
But I promise you this
Unless you have walked in my shoes,
Then you'll never know what I've been through

You can read every poem or chapter
That I've ever written
Just to formulate your own conclusion

But until you have seen life through my eyes,
Then what you thought was comprehension
Will be nothing more than a whole lot of confusion

And for those of you who think
That my head is getting bigger by the day, you're right
Cause I got a head full of big dreams
That keep getting bigger as my eyes stay on the prize

Cause I gotta make sure that I secure my spot beside
Langston Hughes in those literature text books
In the event of my demise

So if you hate to love me now
Then I now that you ain't ready for what I have in store

And I'm sorry if there has been some miscommunication,
So let me take the time now
To let you know who it really is
That God has chosen me to write these words for

These words are for
The kids who get off the school bus hungry
And there is no one even home

These words are for the kids who do bad in school
Because what they don't understand about their
homework, they gotta figure out on their own

These words are for
The little boys and girls who cry out silently
Cause they feel like they ain't got no voice

These words are for
The teenage boys who slang rocks from dust to dawn
Cause they feel like they ain't got no other choice

These words are for college girls who strip late at night
Just to feed their child and to pay their tuition

These words are for
Those who always extend a helping hand
But when they need help, everyone is missing

These words are for those who are now just living to die
And stopped dieing to live

These words are for those who gave it all they had
And feel like they just ain't got no more to give

These words are for all of our fallen soldiers
Who don't even know what it really is
That they was fighting for

These words are for
All the women who've been hurt so bad by men
That they refuse to love again
And now thinks that another women
Won't make her cry anymore

These words are for
All of the men and women who are sitting behind bars
Praying that God allows them to see the day
That they can be free again

These words are for those who lost their lives
In those planes and buildings
So God Bless the family and friends
Of the Victims, The Police, and The Firemen

And if it's Gods will
Then I'll just keep writing these words
Until the Ink runs Dry or I just can't write anymore

And if you don't like it, then too bad
Cause you ain't who I write these words for

Rest In Peace Lil' Bro.

Tomorrow has gone away
And yesterday is just a memory of todays' dearly departed

And now that the future has become the past
We stand in between them both with tears of joy
But at the same time broken hearted

Thinking of the memories is what makes us laugh
But it's the lost that makes us cry

Knowing that in the law of nature this day must come
But yet we ask God why

Not asking God why this must happen
But just why so soon

Thinking of the beautiful rose that grew from concrete
But never had a chance to completely bloom

Win to Lose

It seems to me that even when I win I still Lose
So now I'm confused
And I don't even know which paths to choose

I've tried to make it on my own debt free
So I've paid my dues

I got tired of hearing the same old songs,
So I changed the station
But I find myself still singing the blues

It's like the sky's the limit
But I can't get seem to get off the ground

And it's funny how everyone loves me from 9 –5
But after that no one seems to be around

So how can I win from losing
How can I fight for everything I believe in
Without my motivation bruising

I guess it's like Yen and Yuan, cause there's no Good without Bad
No White without Black, or no Heaven without Hell

I guess that's why I must fall flat on my ass
Before I even have a chance to prevail

They say after the pain comes the pleasure
And after the search comes the treasure

But before you find that pot of gold at the end of the rainbow
You must be able to endure the stormy weather

So how can I win without losing
How can I fight for the love I once had
Without my heart bruising

Cause I couldn't wipe away her tears fast enough
To stop her from crying

I couldn't turn back the hands of time fast enough
To save our only unborn child from dieing

But what can you do
When you ain't even got a pot to pea in

And now she wants to bring a child into this world
To pea into the same pot

That you ain't even got

And now she's mad at you
Because of a decision that you made together

Having to say goodbye before hello
She no longer believes in forever

So how can I win without losing
How can I continue to fight for free expression
Without my inspiration bruising

Cause if I truly speak my mind on how I really feel
Then I'll step on so many toes

And all of the people that supported me through hard times
May slowly change from friends to foes

Because you're not free
Just because you're not bound in shackles and chains

You're still a slave in your on mind
Until you decide to brake free from all the mental games

Cause your slave master is whom or whatever
That holds you back from progression

And no matter if you're black or white you're still a slave
If you continue to live under stress and depression

So that's why I write poetry

That's why I release my mind
Of all of the worlds' negativity

That's why I cleanse my body
Of all of the hate that's held inside of me

But that's the very reason
You want see me in the Newspaper or on TV

So How Can I Win Without Losing?

Off The Stage

Just the other day this little boy said that he wanted to be like me
And I had to catch myself
Because I almost asked him why

He said he admired how I always shined in the spotlight
But I had to explain to him
That everything ain't always what it seems
And just because I smile on the outside
Doesn't mean that on the inside I don't cry

I had to explain to him how it feels to be me
When the crowd leaves
And the venue turns out the light

And how Sean Ingram only gets to be Lil' Sean
For only about 20-30 minutes on any given day or night

But I can see that it's hard for my little man to
comprehend that his boy Lil' Sean also shed tears

And when Lil' Sean goes to sleep at night
His sweet dreams also gets invaded by fears

But it's true, cause when the crowd leaves
Lil' Sean is left alone

Just a scared little boy who fears
That when his Grandma dies he will be left on his own

Because the only person
That he knew loved him unconditionally
Would be forever gone

And everyone else would only love him
When the spotlight would be on

So please don't want to be like me little man
Be yourself and you'll do just fine

Just remember to say your prayers at night
And I'll continue to pray
That your life is better than mine

But it hurt so bad, cause I could see it in his eyes
And I seen that he was just like me

And in time he would become the man
That he thought as a child he always wanted to be

But right now he's still just another lonely child
With nothing in the world to lose

That will one day grow up to become an angry man
That in some way will express his blues

Me and him are one of a kind
So I can feel his pain

Neither does he has anyone at home
So therefor he wanders off to play alone in the rain

And just thinking about it
Put me right back to the beginning of our conversation

Because I then realized
That despite what I've been through in life
That Lil' Sean was this young mans motivation

And as I signed his book

I saw a smile on his face like none I've ever seen before

So I just told him to grow up and make me proud
So one day I can read his book
And say now that's my boy

The Chosen One part2

I watched my whole life pass me by
In the reflection of my grandmothers tears

When the judge announced in the courtroom
That I could be residing in a federal prison
For the next ten to fifteen years

But I didn't cry
I mean why should I

Cause I figure I gotta be on my way to heaven now
Cause I've already been through hell

I've been locked up and shackled down by chains
But they still couldn't stop this caged bird
From singing in his jail cell

Who in the hell think they can stop what's part of Gods plan
Because if God is for me
Then who in the hell can be against me man?

Do you really think I stand on these stages
Night by night just because I think it's cool?
Or maybe you think I like to hear the sound of my own voice

Do you really think I chose to be a poet,
When I could've been a doctor?
Hell no my people, this is Gods plan;
I never even had a choice

See I was chosen to prophecize poetic prophecies
Until God feels my job on earth has been well done

And no matter how many times I try to deny my position
My talents and blessings show me
That I am indeed Gods chosen one

See I was chosen to rewrite and recite scriptures
Until every soul on earth can understand

So that's why I'll die trying to spread my poetic prophesies
By hitting open mics from land to land

But I don't think yall understand what it is that I'm saying

See I told you once before that I am the chosen one,
But not the only one
Because there's a lot of brothers and sisters
Who were chosen to wear my same shoes

From Martin and Tupac to Sheba and The Women Storm
All the way down to the homeless people
That's laying on the corner right now singing the ill street blues

See I myself never chose to become a poetic prophet,
This is Gods will
So that's why I gotta keep speaking these words
Until my last days on earth is done

So just like Malcolm I dropped the little
But I didn't add the X
Because it's not unknown
Why they call me Sean Ingram The Chosen One

But don't get me wrong,
Cause it's cool if you call me Lil' Sean every now and then
Because honestly, I'm still a big kid at heart and mind

But the Bible teaches me that now that I've became a man
I must leave all of my childish ways behind

But see I must admit that it's hard sometimes

Because now matter how old you may get
The hurt child inside of you will still shed tears

And if you're wondering why your sweet dreams
Sometimes turn into nightmares
That's just because you haven't let go of your childhood fears

But I understand

Because I myself have dreams bigger than Martin could imagine
And visions that only me and God can see
But I ain't got time to cry for myself
Cause I'm to busy crying for everybody else that's around me

So I ask you also

Who will cry for the little boy
That cries inside of I

Who will mend my broken heart, wipe away my tears
And show me why it's better to live than to die

Who will ease my heartache and pains
And stand by my side through thick and thin

Who will pick me up and brush me off
And be my crutch just to make sure that I don't fall again

I ask you; Who?

So please look into your mental roladex
And bring forward the first name that comes to your mind

Take a look back into your life
And bring forward the first person that you can find

Who's that person that embraced you
No matter what you may have been going through

Now I can only speak for myself
But I now ain't nobody done for me, what God could do

God has been my mother and my father
When I had no parents in the home

God has been my best friend
When everybody else I cared for left me on my own

God has been my everything
So that's why I gotta keep speaking his words
Until my last days on earth is done

And if I should happen to die tonight
Then I just pray that the world remember the words of
Sean Ingram The Chosen One

Gods' Glory

I know a lot of you may get tired of me always talking spiritual
But to be honest with you
I ain't got much to say if I can't talk about Gods glory

Because those that truly know me
Can tell you that it's a blessing
That I can even stand before you today
And tell you my story

And please believe that I speak from the heart
So therefore I speak the truth
And nothing that I say will be phony

My people
I come to tell you about the grace and mercy of God
Through the words that's in this poem
Or shall I say my testimony

And naw I don't sit in a church pew every Sunday
But when I do, and please believe that I do

It want be to impress you
Or to fit in with you and your crew

And naw I might not jump around and shout
Because I rather sit quietly
And let the preacher teach me What Jesus Would Do

Cause I now realize that I have no future
If I don't have God in my life in the future

Because I'm gonna need God in my future
To get past my devilish past

Cause only God can deliver me
From all of the sins that I have done in my past

And that's why I thank God
Cause I remember when my life was nothing more than a mess

And when I think about where I am now
Compared to where I use to be
I know that I've been blessed

God has blessed me to look into your eyes
And write out the story of your life

I have been blessed to paint poetic portraits in watercolor
Using the tears of the fatherless child
And the blood from the broken heart of the widowed wife

I have been blessed to paint poetic portraits
Of a all of the lost souls
Using the charcoal out of the ashes and dust
Of their hell bound souls

I have been blessed to paint portraits
Of the thugs and hustlers
Who found themselves trapped into the game
Because they found themselves chasing all of the wrong goals

I've been please to paint poetic portraits with my tongue
Just as Van Gough was blessed to paint art

I've been blessed to touch the hearts of the misguided youth
Cause they know that I speak from the heart

They know that I will never forsake them
Until death do us part

And even when I die I'll still be with them
Cause just like Pac
They'll forever carry me in their heart

Cause they know
That nobody wrote it quit like I

And they know
That nobody brought the words to life quit like I

And they know
That nobody could stand on a stage and quote it quit like I

Cause nobody took the words right out of their mouth
And spit it through the wire quit like I

And know that I will never stop
Until my heart stop

And even when my heart stop
The seeds that I have sowed in life
Will continue to grow through concrete non-stop

My grandma always told me that I should slow down
Before I work my young self to death

But I told her that I got souls to touch
So I won't rest until I'm resting in peace
And I won't stop speaking
Until I breathe my last breath

My people I can see clearly now
Now that my tears have washed out my eyes

Can't you see the twinkle in my eyes
Now that I have my eyes on the sparrow
And now that I have my eyes on the prize

Can't you see the smile on my face
I mean don't it put a smile on your face
To see the under dog at the head of the race

And I know that the devil don't want me to win
But I aint worried about him taking my prize
Because God said what's mine is mine

And I refuse to let him or anybody else knock me off track
Cause I refuse to lose this time around
Because this time, heaven is my finish line

Also Available by Sean Ingram

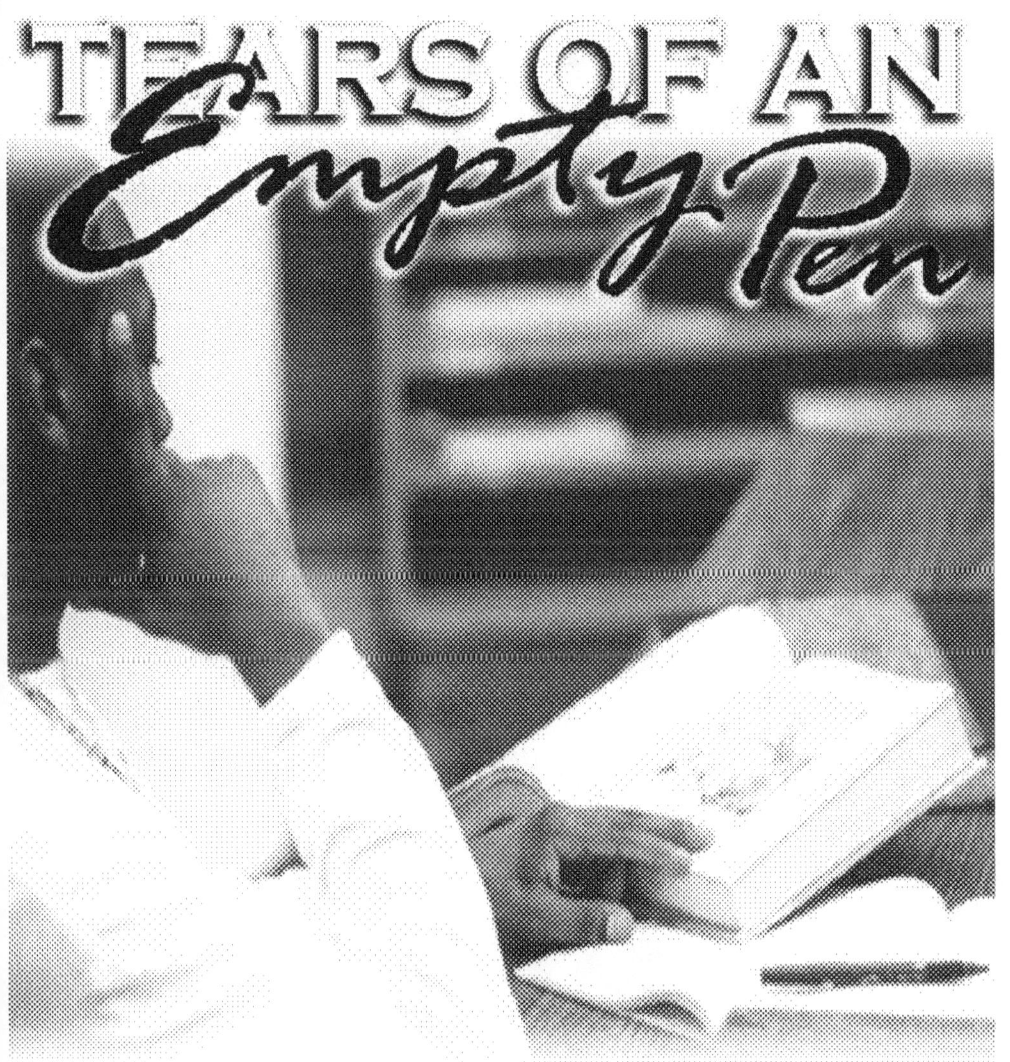

SEAN INGRAM

ISBN 0-615-11910-7

www.ingramcontent.com/pod-product-compliance
Lightning Source LLC
Chambersburg PA
CBHW022147050726
47590CB00002B/592